My Travels With Footsbarn Theatre

the
liffey
press

Published by
The Liffey Press
'Clareville', 307 Clontarf Road
Dublin D03 PO46, Ireland
www.theliffeypress.com

© 2025 Ted Turton

A catalogue record of this book is
available from the British Library.

ISBN 978-1-0686645-4-0

Printed in Northern Ireland by W&G Baird

MY TRAVELS WITH FOOTSBARN THEATRE

A Memoir

Ted Turton

The Liffey Press

Contents

Foreword by President Michael D. Higgins   vii

Read This First   1

Run Away, Run Away!   3

In the Beginning: Footsbarn Theatre Comes to Ireland   5

Turning Up the Heat   17

The Nature of the Barnstorming Theatre Company I Had Joined   19

Spain, September 1981   25

Theatre on the Beach   29

Portugal, a Base Camp and a New Show, 1981–82   36

The Devil, The Doctor and The Fool   42

On the Road Again   47

America, July 1982   52

A Day in Manhattan   55

Back to Portugal   62

The Story of Phil Oldaker   66

Lisbon   70

Spain Again   73

Skin-deep in Jerez   78

The Great Escape – An Epic Journey Across Spain   82

1983: The Year I Always Wanted   87

Siena and Volterra   91

The King Lear Poster   97

Avignon and the Palais des Papes   104

Pisa   109

Lucia   112

A Home in France   118

Back in Galway   126

Julie   131

Western Australia, February 1985   135

A Blast (Furnace) from the Past   145

South Australia   147

The Top End and Its Aboriginal Communities   151

Bali, Indonesia   158

Queensland   165

Ups and Downs along the Pacific Coast   169

Christmas in Melbourne, New Year in Sydney   174

Macbeth, Something Wicked   175

Back in Europe, 1986   181

The Base Camp at Creepy Belbezet   185

Italy in the Fall and France through the Winter   189

And Finally, The End Bit   193

Members of the Company, 1981-1987   198

Photo Gallery   199

Footsbarn Theatre Itinerary, May 1981 – May 1987   202

Picture Gallery   205

Acknowledgements   213

Foreword

President Michael D. Higgins

As President of Ireland, I have had the privilege of witnessing the power of the arts and culture in bringing people from diverse backgrounds together, and of the resonance and the transcendence made possible by art. Ted Turton's experiences with the travelling Footsbarn Theatre serve as a tribute to artistic passion and as a shining example of the profound impact that artists and cultural practitioners can have on both the individual and society.

Traveling across Europe, Ted and his group embodied the true essence of collaboration and inclusivity, using theatre to challenge norms and connect cultures. In today's world, this story serves as an evocative reminder that the arts can be a bridge between cultures, fostering understanding and unity in a world that now finds itself divided and in conflict.

Having served as Mayor of Galway on two occasions and as a former Minister for Culture, I recall taking great pride and delight in Footsbarn's longstanding involvement in the Galway Arts Festival, such a successful contribution to the community which greatly enriched the local artistic and cultural scene. Ted's posters for the

Galway Arts Festival were just fabulous. Now collector's items, I have one that I treasure.

May I commend Ted for this work which serves as an inspiration to embrace exploration, creativity, and create a society without bounds for artistic expression. This account of a journey across the planet also reveals a deep and generous humanity, openness to vulnerability and a resilience to which so many regularly look to artists for reminder.

Michael D. Higgins
Uachtaráin na hÉireann
President of Ireland

This book is dedicated to all the Footsbarn children.
Thank you all for your help and the fun you shared with me.

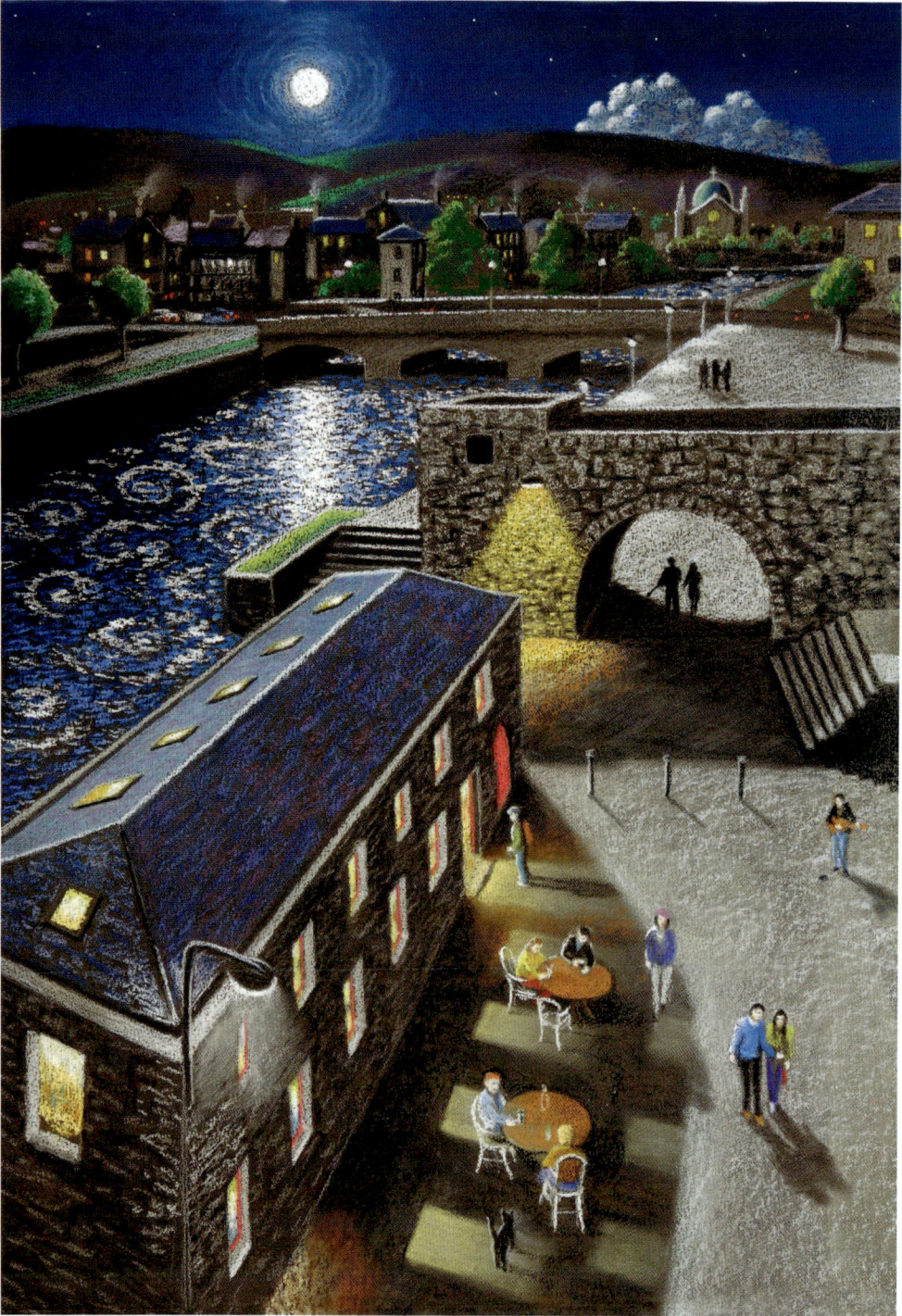

Spanish Arch, Galway

Read This First

It's more than just a disclaimer.

This is not so much a book about theatre and acting. It is a memoir about travelling with a theatre company, which was a drama in itself. It does include descriptions of the kind of theatre that Footsbarn were engaged in, but only to set the scene, so to speak, especially for those of you who are unfamiliar with this extraordinary group of travelling players.

This book represents my personal memories, views and opinions and does not necessarily reflect the positions or opinions of any organisation or individual with which I am associated, past or present. Nor does it represent the views of Footsbarn Theatre or its members. These stories are true only in as much as they are my memories from a long time ago. To those of you I write about, you who were there with Footsbarn as part of its ever-evolving journey, I am so grateful for your friendship and appreciation. I have not, in any way, intended to offend or misrepresent you and what you achieved. This is especially pertinent to the Footsbarn administration in general and John Kilby in particular. The job John did was awesome, in my opinion: he was always in pursuit of making the desires of the whole group happen and coming up with possibilities to further the cause. If I am critical of what choices we made as a group, it should not reflect on him as administrator.

You were all a fabulous inspiration to me. If you remember differently the things I write about, I totally understand, and I apologise if some details are inaccurate or misplaced. One or two people's names have been changed to protect their privacy. I have used first names in the narrative because it seems friendlier. All the personnel are listed at the back of the book. Some of them hardly get a mention in the text even though they might have been my favourites.

Footsbarn's story is a long one, and this is just a small part of it. To Paddy and Freddy, who carry the torch for the company now, I say: Long may it continue, God bless you, and all my love to you and those who might remember me.

This IS a disclaimer: Neither the publisher nor any associated parties shall be held responsible for any consequences arising from the opinions or interpretations expressed within this book.

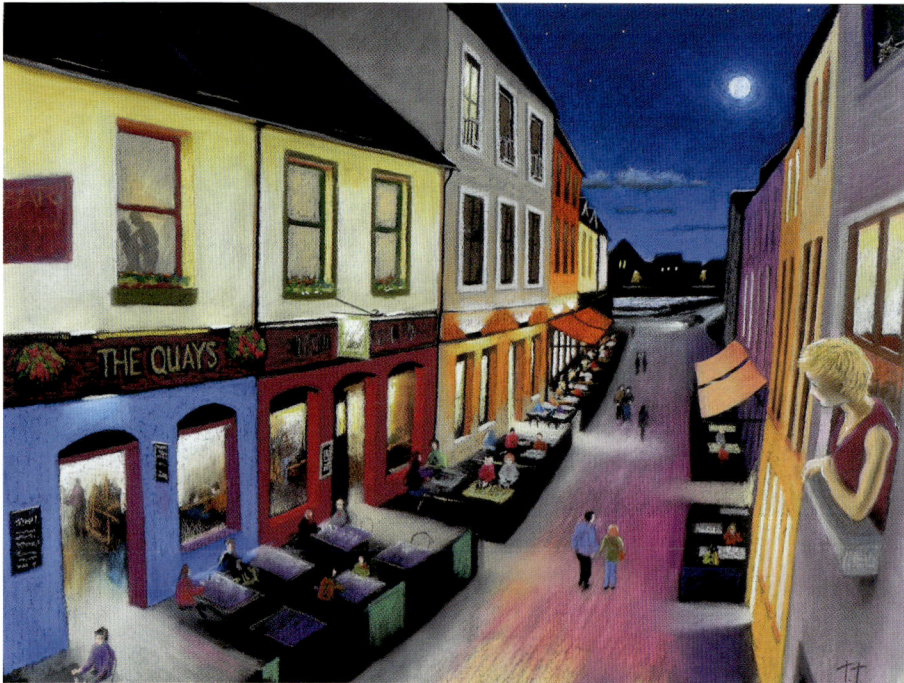

Quay Street, Galway

Run Away, Run Away!

Although I missed them when Footsbarn Theatre first visited Galway in summer 1979 because I was working in New York, I met and got to know the group a little later when they performed *Hamlet* at the Galway Arts Festival in 1981. Footsbarn had a big impact on Galway back then, and subsequently on the alternative theatre scene right across Europe. The show they performed in Galway in their own tent in August 1979, called *Arthur*, based on the legendary King Arthur and the Knights of the Round Table, was screamingly funny and typical of their *commedia dell'arte* style. But it was their version of Shakespeare's *Hamlet* in 1981 that really turned the theatre world on its head.

These first visits to Ireland prompted a long love affair between this barnstorming company of extraordinarily talented performers, actors, clowns, acrobats, musicians, artists, technicians and all their children, on one hand, and the good people of Galway and Ireland on the other, who in turn were hospitable and friendly, way beyond normal measure, as well as being enthralled and inspired.

Footsbarn's free-spirited nature and boisterous energy, together with a rough and ready can-do attitude, attracted many talented people who yearned to join up and run away with the company, or wished they were free to do so. The notion of taking theatre to the people, be it in the city, the suburbs or rural communities, was romantically attractive. The reality was a tough, 24/7 life on the road with trucks, buses, travelling school and tents, including the main theatre tent, all of which had to be maintained, repaired and kept going relentlessly. This was showbiz in a modern version of what circuses and travelling players had been doing for centuries. Fortunately, the mental and physical toughness required to do it directly influenced Footsbarn's theatrical style.

The company's brilliant understanding of how to deliver tragedy and comedy matched their limitless inventive and creative talents. Audiences came away from a Footsbarn show enchanted with a taste of the exotic and aching inside from laughter, the kind of laughter that threatened your bodily functions. Moments later, you could be reeling from scenes of pathos that rent your heart or, having witnessed acts of murder and savage cruelty within touching distance, you were left wondering if you had ever enjoyed being so terrified before. The agony and the ecstasy were shovelled in spadefuls.

THIS IS THE COMPANY I JOINED AS an artist, designer, photographer, printer, admin assistant, truck driver, publicist, front-of-house salesperson, document forger, occasional street actor and general dogsbody. I was just thirty-one. This book is about how I ran away with the circus, travelled the world with a crazy, infuriating, endearing and totally inspirational family of many nationalities and the children who came with us. The stories include some of the scrapes I got into, the adventures I had in the places we visited and several tales about the characters in the travelling group. It is illustrated with the work I did as an artist while with the company and some of the photographs I took with a 1970s Leica M2 rangefinder camera, my constant companion.

The author circa 1981

In the Beginning: Footsbarn Theatre Comes to Ireland

Anyone who saw Footsbarn Theatre on their first visit to Ireland from their home in Cornwall, back in the summer of 1979, can count themselves lucky, as those happy few were treated to an extraordinary display of barnstorming comedy. The company's small theatre tent, accommodating an audience of little more than two hundred, went up on the circus site at Booterstown in Dublin, followed by a few days on Fisheries Field in Galway city and finally on the show grounds in Clifden before they packed up and returned to base. It was the first time that Fisheries Field, next to the salmon weir, was used as a tent site, with the kind permission of the University of Galway (then University College Galway). The same site is still used by the Galway International Arts Festival for all its Big Top events.

That first presentation in Ireland was a show called *Arthur*, a tragicomic tale of the legendary king with a dubious assortment of knights in search of a quest. And I missed it! I was in New York that summer, working in the offices of an art magazine publisher on the twenty-ninth floor of a skyscraper on Madison Avenue in Manhattan. When my visa expired and the summer ran out of steam, I returned to Galway, where all my friends were talking about this crazy Cornish theatre company that had taken the place by storm. They left nothing behind except for a few broken hearts, a bag full of memories and a patch of dead grass on Fisheries Field where the Footsbarn tent had been erected.

For some Galwegians, their lives had been changed utterly. How could a troupe of barnstormers doing a tragicomic show about King Arthur have such a transforming effect? I found out for myself several months later when I saw Footsbarn's version of *The Golden Fleece* at the Project Arts Centre in Dublin. Irresistibly appealing to

Ted's first poster for Footsbarn

young people, the humour was side splitting, the theatrical craft high-ly inventive, the performances physically demanding and energetic and it was all completely bonkers. I was spellbound and could hardly wait for their next visit to Ireland, when Ollie Jennings invited them to perform Shakespeare's *Hamlet* for the 1981 Galway Arts Festival.

If *Arthur* had been an appetiser, then *Hamlet* was a feast. A much more mature show than the previous presentations in Ireland, *Hamlet* was full of sleight-of-hand theatrical tricks, bold African-influenced costumes, acrobatics, outrageous comedy and murderous devilment.

From the very beginning, the moment when the actors ran full pelt along the aisles and pole-vaulted onto the stage, raising the ghost of Hamlet's father above them so that he hovered magically over the creeping mist, the entire audience was caught up in a collective trance. We all instantly forgot about our uncomfortable bench seats and the meagre circus-tent surroundings and lapped up every drop of juice those actors and musicians dished up. It left everyone wanting more.

A black and white photo of the Hamlet show by Pete Smith that
I coloured using a posterisation technique for a publicity brochure

It wasn't as if we were bereft of decent theatrical experiences here in Galway. I had been privileged to work with the Druid Theatre in the 1970s when they were laying down a marker for innovative theatre on a scale beyond expectations. My own theatrical awakening (if you exclude my Dad's amateur dramatics in the local church hall) had begun with an experience in Paris in 1975, when a friend took me to see Ariane Mnouchkine's company Théâtre du Soleil performing *L'Âge d'Or* (*The Golden Age*) in an open-plan promenade setting at their theatre warehouse, a former munitions factory in Vincennes. I knew from then on that no matter what the movies or television threw at me, it was not going to match the assault on the senses that this live experience served up right in front of my eyes.

Though many of Footsbarn's actors had been trained in Paris by Jacques Lecoq, their shows were in English, so there was an added charm and easy accessibility that endeared them to me. The text was abridged to suit the company's style of performance, but it was true to the spirit of the play. 'If Shakespeare was turning in his grave,' as one critic put it, 'it was only so he could get a better view.'

So when I eventually met Footsbarn as a company of extraordinary people in Galway that spring of 1981, and finally got to experience what this cult following was all about, it was the first time I had the chance to get up close and personal with any of the group members. And there were lots of them.

The day they all arrived in Ireland in their trucks and buses just happened to be Good Friday, so after the long haul across the country and an hour or so establishing camp on Galway's Fisheries Field, there was much consternation and dismay when they were told that this was one of the few days in the Irish calendar when you couldn't get any alcohol as all the pubs and off licences were closed. It was the one day of the year that many pub landlords chose to give the interior walls a lick of paint or scrape the nicotine off the ceiling.

An arrangement with the owners of the Quays Bar for a private, albeit illicit, party behind closed shutters saved the day from disaster. At least it did for a couple of hours until the effort of trying to keep conversation to a whisper went beyond the capabilities of any self-respecting inebriated group of young people. The keenest members of An Garda Síochána, who were roaming the dark streets of Galway in full knowledge that there must be rich pickings around here somewhere, had the whole lot of us busted and everybody's names taken. Addresses were duly supplied, such as third caravan on the left, Fisheries Field, down the lane after the Salmon Weir bridge. So a good start to the world tour then.

Sometime later, in the kitchen of the three-storey apartment I shared with friends at the end of Shop Street in the heart of Galway, a fragment of the party continued in a more boisterous manner. Two of the Footsbarn performers were there, with several others from the group, along with a host of my mates, all jammed into the available standing spaces around the kitchen table. Endless cups of tea and a few precious donated bottles of wine kept the party going until Paddy and Warwick, who I hardly knew, decided to do one of their show tricks.

Adopting their clown show characters and making a great fuss of shushing everyone present, Paddy then produced a huge old fashioned copper penny from his pocket and asked Warwick to assume the position, bending forward slightly so that Paddy could lodge the penny securely between the cheeks of his bum. Or should I say, it was somewhere discreetly hidden in the folds of Warwick's industrial strength trousers. You get the picture. With this coin in place Paddy added a firework, a banger, asking 'strong man' Warwick to clench it tightly so that the blue touch paper was still visible. With a great flourish Paddy set fire to the banger and stood back. Wondering if he was really going to do this, we all immediately took evasive action and cowered with our ears covered, just about in time, before the banger went off in a cloud of smoke and the most incredible clap of thunder, contained as it was within the walls of the tiny kitchen. Warwick staggered around the room pushing astonished people out of the way, and with eyes as big as saucers, he coughed up the penny into the

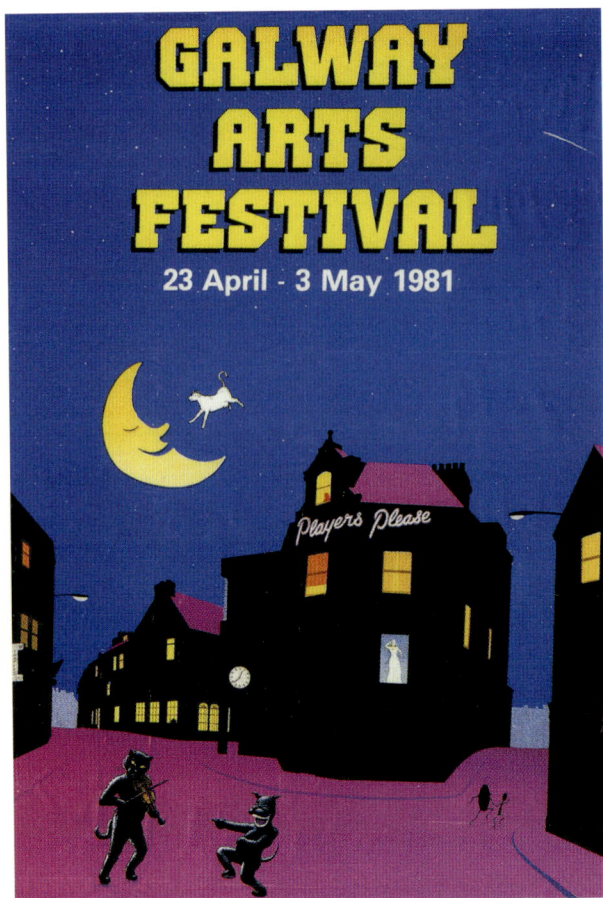

Poster for Galway Arts Festival, 1981

sink. After the hilarity had died down it was clear that this signalled the end of the party because no one could hear anybody else's muffled voice due to the ringing sound in their ears. Everyone spilled out of the building and into the quiet April night air and went home, still shaking their heads, still chuckling, still trying to adjust the ring tone. This was my first close encounter with the Footsbarn performers and one I was unlikely to forget.

THAT APARTMENT IS IMMORTALISED IN THE 1981 Galway Arts Festival poster. I had introduced the characters of the 'Hey diddle diddle' nursery rhyme to Shop Street where they frolicked in the small hours of the night. My room, in the attic where I also had a small studio, is above the Players Please neon advertising sign. I included the sign in the poster even though it had been years since the light actually worked, because I thought it neatly referred to the 'players' on the street rather than the brand of cigarettes it famously advertised. The kitchen, referred to earlier, was on the first floor behind the bride manikin in the window. She was always lit up at night, reminding us that her boutique was in the shop below at street level. The poster was popular not least because it was our first attempt to print a poster in four colours for the festival, which was extravagant at the time. Standard printers in Shantalla in Galway did a brilliant job printing two colours at a time so we didn't know how it would turn out until the final black colour went down and pulled everything together.

One of the Footsbarn technicians who had asked for a copy of the poster to decorate his truck conversion to a home for the road came back beaming with delight to tell me that his infant son Danny had pointed at the poster from his high chair and said his first word – 'moon'! For some reason, this pleased me more than any art critic's review and since Danny now works in London's West End it's nice to know that it must have been a positive influence for the little fellow at the beginning of his life's journey.

Within a month I had joined the company as we left our homes behind and set off on a preposterous world tour. It proved to be a six-year adventure that would shape the rest of my life.

WHEN I SAY I RAN AWAY WITH THE CIRCUS, it was almost by accident: I left Galway intending to return to New York, where I'd been offered work on an animated film. I had made a clumsy attempt to join Footsbarn while the final shows were still going on in Galway by suggesting to John Kilby in the Quays Bar over a pint of Guinness that the company needed someone like me. I had even promised that I would effectively pay for myself by creating more revenue through poster and programme sales than they would have to cough up in wages. It was a nice try, but John said that he was concerned about paying the personnel they already had and what it would take to keep the show on the road after abandoning their base in Cornwall.

The company headed off for Brittany while I prepared to pack up my Galway life after four great years, with the optimistic hope that I would be able to get back into America to work. However, knowing their next stop after Brittany was going to be in Amsterdam, I couldn't resist dropping in to see 'Footies' on the way (well, sort of on the way) in one of their natural habitats, the Vondelpark in the centre of Amsterdam, where they had been invited to set up the theatre tent. I was especially keen to see one of the administrators I'd befriended in Galway. Eva hadn't been with the company long, but she spoke six languages which had been a real asset to them as they set out touring Europe.

Eva, Fisheries Field, Galway – Henry was fixing a huge dent in the truck after an argument with a large horse chestnut tree

Getting a surprisingly warm reception from everyone when I turned up in Amsterdam, especially from Eva, I thought I'd stick around for a few days.

Ironically, it was John who immediately put me to work hand-printing silk screen posters of the *Arthur* show in a back room of the famous *Melkweg* (Milky Way) cafe. After that I was printing leaflets and handing them out around a city I barely knew.

There was a European-wide youth culture beyond Dublin and London, it seemed, that I was completely unaware of, full of strange delights like 'Jango Edwards' and 'Fools on the Road', and Amsterdam was a beacon for it all. At the time there was a jaunty hit song that everyone in the nightclubs loved to get up and dance to, singing along with the chorus, and of course I joined in, singing, 'I'm still down, I'm still down'. Eva asked what on earth was I singing? She said the correct lyrics were 'Amsterdam, Amsterdam', but hey, what did I care, I was young enough to feel that the world was my oyster, and I just wanted to swallow it whole. Did anyone really care about what I was singing? No, of course not. I was getting a taste for the bright lights of continental Europe, so I raised a glass to this wonderful city, got the words right and just kept dancing.

My joining Footsbarn happened to coincide with the company's own reverse Brexit. Through the 1970s the company had been based in Cornwall, creating shows there and touring from that base. In 1981 they abandoned their British home with the aim of going permanently on the road with their trucks and buses and theatre tent, including all the children and a travelling school, administrators, a costumier, technicians, musicians, and even a mechanic to keep the show going. Surprisingly, a British Council grant made it possible. At least, it did in the beginning, supporting what had been ambitiously dubbed 'a five-year world tour'.

Just when I was getting to know Eva, who was originally from Germany, she went off to Switzerland to work with a film company for a few weeks, saying we would catch up again in Avignon in July.

*1981-82 Tour of western Europe, not exactly as it
was planned but as it turned out*

In June the company moved on to Freiburg in the Black Forest region
of southern Germany. I was used to German girls, as I had lived with
one in the late 1970s in Galway, but this was my first experience of
Germany the country. Eva left me with two of her girlfriends at a flat
in the pleasantly leafy Freiburg town centre. It was kind of them to
have me stay, because I had no travelling accommodation of my own,
not even a tent. And at this stage, I still wasn't sure if the company
was going to take me on, as I'd had no official invitation to join up.

I set to work translating articles and reviews from the German
newspapers. I was struggling with one at the kitchen table when the

phone rang in the corridor, right in front of the open kitchen door. Unsure if either of the two women were in their rooms, I glared at the phone with the intention of making it stop ringing, when one of the women suddenly appeared. Christiana was in her late twenties, tall, with blonde hair and striking blue eyes. She was classically beautiful, with a friendly, open face; she and her handsome boyfriend, whom I had met at a gathering the previous evening, made a gorgeous couple. She answered the phone completely naked and sat facing me, legs crossed on a little seat next to a low table.

This wasn't exactly comfortable for me. I felt pinned to the kitchen table and was wondering whether this might be a regular German custom with strange visitors in the house. Though I was a shy rather than a brash or bold type, I couldn't help looking up at her occasionally, admiring the long legs, as an artist you understand, but the thought of brushing past her to get to my room, forcing her to stand up, was not on my option list at this point, even after twenty minutes. It would have been a little risky of me to presume that it was on *her* agenda, so I sat it out even though my work was long completed. But wait: the need to relieve some of my breakfast was gaining urgency. After I gave the newspaper a few loud shakes, turning it inside out, she took the hint, put the phone back on the hook and gracefully disappeared.

Life on the road was already throwing up challenges and revealing priorities; after all, I needed the room more than I needed another girlfriend. My introduction to European life, and how different it was from nine years of living in Ireland, was proving to be starkly shocking. A visit to the red-light district in Amsterdam the previous week with one of my new Footsbarn actor friends had been enlightening, so to speak. We were treated to a bewildering array of exotic images through street-level windows so close to your face that you felt the blood rushing to your body's extremities without the need to step inside the building and get more involved. Bear in mind that I was coming from 1970s Ireland, where church and state had colluded to produce a double dose of social *repression* and economic *depression*, and the regime had somehow convinced its population that God wasn't entirely sure that sex was a good thing.

In Freiburg, I got an idea of just how tough life on the road could be when one of the children, Rebecca, collided with a moving car on her bicycle and broke her leg. She came back from the hospital thigh to toe in plaster. That was coupled with *föhn* winds that came down from the Alps, said by the locals to bring on headaches, migraines, depression and deafening thunderstorms that would shake the mountains out of their summer slumbers and drench everything that wasn't safely under canvas – all of which came to pass and was evidence enough that this was no holiday. However, we were also treated to gifts of so many baskets of fresh cherries from generous local people that we hardly knew what to do with them after a week of gorging.

Rebecca H with her leg in plaster

An unexpected boon and a feature of the wealth of West Germany, as it was then, was the day of the month when unwanted household items were put out on the street for collection came around. Most of us managed to raid this street larder before the council workers turned up, so that things like electric hair driers, kitchen implements, washing machines in perfect working order and furniture small enough to fit in a bus or caravan vanished before dawn broke. In fact, everything was fair game, including the kitchen sink!

Turning Up the Heat

As we moved on to Avignon in the south of France, I was told that the invitation to perform at its prestigious festival was the biggest gig in the company's ten-year history. When we set up on a dry and dusty site on the edge of the city, I got my first taste of intense heat and yet another local wind. This one, the mistral, was a hot wind that blew for three days and sometimes six.

Before Eva returned, I was faced with a dilemma. Dave H approached me one afternoon after the company had had a group meeting. The good news, he said, was that I'd been invited to join the company, but the bad news was that they had decided to fire Eva for not being there when the company had needed her most. She took it well and bought me a chromatic harmonica before we said a sad farewell and off she went to settle in Amsterdam.

I bought my first tent and geared myself up as best I could for a life on the road. I worked away in baking heat, making new banners, sign-writing some of the trucks, and decorating the big bass drum, all in a new typeface that I invented for the company.

The French daily newspapers like *Le Figaro*, *Libération* and *Le Monde*, and the weekly *L'Express*, were full of rave reviews for our performances, so publicity was more a question of doing interviews than a hard sell. The complete run of

Footsbarn letterhead

shows sold out easily, and we had a big party on the day off. A journalist came down to the site one afternoon when I was trying to teach myself how to juggle. He had a photographer with him, so we had to arrange something for him to photograph, and because there was no one on site apart from myself and Rod, who was the lead actor in *Hamlet*, the pictures in the newspaper the following day were of me juggling, me sitting at a typewriter in front of a truck and Rod sitting on his bed looking like Adonis. What a joke! This was my first press interview for the company, and somehow I'd managed to monopolise the whole story.

Oh, but the food! In contrast to rural Ireland's grocery shops in those days, where you often had only one kind of cheese to buy, usually sliced and processed, here in France there was a different cheese for each day of the year. I hid in the supermarkets during the hottest times of the day, chancing the great outdoors again in the late afternoon, but even then, walking out through the supermarket doors was like walking into an oven. We had to distribute paper plates for the audience before the shows started so that they could fan their faces, and we made sure the tent walls were rolled up so that some semblance of cooling air could pass through.

The Nature of the Barnstorming Theatre Company I Had Joined

Footsbarn was an actors' collective, with no single director. It was initially conceived by Oliver Foot and John Paul Cook at the end of the 1960s, and the first shows were in 1971 in Ollie Foot's barn on a property owned by Tom Wildy in Trewen, Cornwall. It had a huge influence on European theatre through the final decades of the twentieth century. Many of the actors were trained by Jacques Lecoq at his famous school in Paris. Lecoq was a master of the study of human physical gestures and archetypes, and his teaching embodied mask work, *commedia dell'arte* and mime techniques. He encouraged his students to adopt a passionate and physically robust attitude to acting and to consider looking at animal behaviour as well as human body language in their studies. He died in 1999 but the school in Paris survived until 2023, and many Irish actors have trained there.

Kids' lunch at Les Marronniers, Aix en Provence

Our actors were contemporaries of Julie Taymor, one of the school's most illustrious pupils, before she went on to study puppetry and mask-making in Indonesia, eventually creating her masterpiece, *The Lion King*, for the stage.

I'm sometimes asked if I acted on stage with Footsbarn. The basic answer is no, although I did get involved with street parades and publicity stunts, and occasionally worked large puppets.

The actors had a range of skills I truly admired, and had I been more extroverted I may have thrown myself on to the stage. But there was a fundamental difference between me and the performers. For example, I was talking to Margaret one day when I happened to pull a funny face, making her burst ino laughter. Straight away she said, 'Now do it again.' And there she had me. I knew I could clown around with the best of them, but doing it time after time and at will is a real art. And, in truth, I was just as happy in a supporting role as long as my skills as an artist were appreciated enough to keep me involved with the company.

Actors Margaret and Dave in St. Siffret, France

Some of these actors were world-class clowns as well as Shakespearean and character actors. They were physically robust and agile and used to living a hard life on the road, putting up the tent in all weathers and making sure it was tied down in the middle of the night whenever a storm blew up. Everyone pitched in, even if as individuals we had our specialist skills; on occasion it was a case of 'all hands to the pumps', and no one was allowed to be too precious about it. The company members enjoyed their reputation for being survivors with a can-do attitude, and wherever they went, their sense of comedy, pathos and sheer *joie de vivre* had a universal appeal.

Footsbarn's depiction of tragedy and violence wouldn't work half so well without the side-splitting comic turns in between. The audience finds it difficult to stay on one level of emotion for any length of time before tuning out. Giving people comic relief or some small uplifting moments allows them to breathe and makes them more willing to follow a character's emotional journey, even if the story contains violence or cruelty and ends in tears or devastation, as *Hamlet* does.

Shakespeare included these moments of relief in his plays because he knew what his audiences could take. Footsbarn enacted their Shakespeare adaptations, preferring to chop bits out of the text rather than change the rhythm and dynamics of the play. The gravediggers scene in Footsbarn's *Hamlet* was hilarious because it happened behind staging that was only two feet high, yet the three Dereks, as they were called, made us believe they were coming up the ladder out of a deep grave. Even though the audience *knew* the 'long' ladder was probably just a short prop, they howled when the ladder tipped backwards and it looked as if the gravedigger might fall because they delighted in the illusion. A lot of Footsbarn's theatrical illusions were simple tricks, sometimes the simpler the better.

Another example from *Hamlet*, during the play within the play, had the audience gasp out loud as a slender baton, not much more than a foot in length, magically hung in the air when the actor let go of it. Another actor's black gloved hand whose finger the baton delicately rested on for the two seconds required to complete the illusion was completely missed by the audience with clever lighting.

The poster for *Hamlet* was a sublime silkscreen print designed by Charett Dykes senior. His son Denis, not much more than a teenager at the time, came to work with Footsbarn on many occasions to do the sign writing on the caravans with circus-style lettering and artwork. The poster included the 'perchance to dream' quotation which was a nice touch, but the omission of the complete text of the 'To be or not to be' soliloquy in the actual performance caused quite a stir.

The actors felt that a Footsbarn Shakespeare show should flow with a certain amount of energy and that the famous soliloquy might be too much contemplation and not enough action. Its soliloquy may well be one of the great dilemmas posed in the English language, and it probably mirrors the equally engrossing scene described in the *Bhagavad Gita* when the warrior archer, Arjuna, asks Krishna how he should act, facing as he does members of his own family across the battlefield. Krishna stops time so that he can instruct Arjuna in the nature of duty and fulfilling his purpose by taking action without worrying too much about the outcome.

Hamlet isn't afforded the same kind of assistance in Shakespeare's play so he is left to consider suicide as a way of escaping his dilemma. In the event, I think Footsbarn got it right and took Krishna's advice, choosing to *act* and in so doing fend off the slings and arrows of outraged theatre critics at the time.

FOOTSBARN'S CLOWN SHOW, *The Circus Tosov*, became something of a blessing and a curse. It was always popular, but it was performed so often that it could be a little 'tired' sometimes. Efforts to spice it up or drop it altogether were always a topic of contention within the group. But when it was good, it was an absolute scream. It was a showcase for the company's talents for buffoonery as well as their love of music, along with a vast array of instruments including Simon's full drum kit. Built around a mock circus (without animals)

Another black and white photo hand-coloured for a Circus Tosov poster

the show consisted of a series of gags, silly tricks that were designed to go right or hilariously wrong, a levitation act, a human cannon and lots of musical interludes including Steve's wobbly carpenter's saw played with a bow.

The evening *Tosov* show evolved into a full blown musical event led by the Rockin' Tossers whose members were the same clown characters, only vamped up to deliver a more bawdy show for adult audiences, which usually went down a treat, especially in Spain and Portugal and in venues where dancing could be encouraged.

Having seen *The Circus Tosov* show more than thirty times I tended to laugh at the things that didn't normally happen. I remember one time at a festival in Santarcangelo in Italy, we were doing an open-air show on a lovely warm summer evening when a small section of the stage collapsed, leaving a gaping hole in the middle of the performing area. I hung around for a while to see if they needed help or to pause the show while the stage was fixed. But no, they just carried on, and the hole became an opportunity for yet more ridiculous buffoonery. Sometimes the actors avoided it, sometimes they fell into it, and the more it happened, the funnier it got.

*Circus Tosov clown show. Bobby Bullethead (Paddy)
and Ronnie Conker (Rod)*

*Circus Tosov – Cyril (Joe) keeps a tight grip
on the elastic with his teeth*

A young couple seated in front of me watched with gaping amazement as Paddy, in character as Bobby Bullethead, was making the most of the chance for more pratfalls. Soon they were doubled over from laughing, and every time they attempted to look up at the action on stage, the sight of Bobby's silly face popping up from inside the hole sent them into another round of hysterics. Clambering out of the hole, Bobby was apologising to Hubert, the master of ceremonies (played by Dave wearing a top-hat that had seen better days) who was himself struggling to keep a straight face. At this point, the two young Italians had tears streaming down their contorted faces and were showing signs of distress as they clutched their aching chests, hardly able to breathe. One more brave glimpse at the events on stage sent them over the edge and, as they capitulated, I watched them slide off their seats to the ground, where they pawed at each other as if they were going down in quicksand, wheezing and coughing like chain-smokers. By the time Ronnie's elastic band attached to a brick gag concluded when Cyril, the brick's intended victim, let go of the elastic from the grip of his teeth and Ronnie got the full twenty feet of stretched elastic tape smack in the face and fell down the hole, I was in tears myself. It had been a classic show.

Spain, September 1981

The first time I set foot in Spain, I threw up. It happened again a year later. I don't know why I had such a physical reaction to Spain – each time it would last only twenty-four hours, and I'd be fine after that – but maybe it set me up to have a love–hate relationship with the place. Consequently, the tales that I tell here are either tinted or tainted accordingly.

We had been doing shows in Foix in the French Pyrenees in early September. The trees were already turning colour and it was getting cooler. We were still doing tent shows, and we needed to move south. My fondness for Foix is due largely to the family I stayed with

Melly, Wanda, Gregg and Joao in front of
The Brute, Sitges, Spain

the week before the rest of the company arrived. I was introduced to a charming woman with eight-year-old identical twin daughters, in whose house I had been given a room because she was a friend of the Foix theatre director. She explained that there wasn't a husband around; she had last seen him when they were living happily in Chile when the girls were little. Pinochet was in power, and one day her university professor husband disappeared and she never saw him again, nor did she hear anything about what had happened to him. He was one of many who disappeared during that regime. Returning to France didn't make things much better, she said, as the immigration authorities in France, her country of birth, refused to believe her story and questioned the validity of the children's right to remain in the country. It must have been an awful burden to live with, but she seemed to be managing in both body and spirit. The girls made me laugh. They loved to go down to the local open-air swimming baths, where one girl would pay to get in, have a swim and then come out, saying she'd forgotten something. A few minutes later her twin would walk in, saying, 'Hi, it's me, I'm back' and get in for free. Half an hour later they would be at the local shop buying stuff with the money they'd saved.

I left France with John Kilby, our administrator, and his dog Brillo, a magnificent long-haired border collie with such a sweet nature that you just wanted to throw your arms round him. The three of us piled into John's truck and headed off higher into the mountains. The easiest way to get to Spain was to go over the top of the Pyrenees via the tiny independent state of Andorra, which was little more than a giant duty-free shop in the sky. I don't think I had ever been as high on terra firma before, and I couldn't have foreseen the depth and intensity of just how blue the colour could be at this level with one's feet still on earth. Artists can be delighted by simple things, and this was one of them. Hey, John Lennon, you were right – the blue of the sky does blow your mind if you are in the right place at the right time.

As we descended from the Pyrenees, the heat increased so that by the time we arrived in Barcelona it was hot, tee-shirt weather again. And what did we find? The bin men were on strike, and the stench from rotting refuse was suffocating as huge piles of trash littered every street. The site itself was a recently demolished abattoir, Parc de l'Escorxador, once rat-infested but now just a city square with a dusty patch of baked earth in the middle. It wasn't a promising prospect and, like I said, I spent the first day vomiting. Years later I rediscovered the place totally transformed into a beautiful park and museum dedicated to the artist Joan Miró. But back in 1981 we were sharing the place with Cirque Aligre, a punk circus troupe from Paris whose tent occupied the opposite corner.

If Footsbarn, as a travelling troupe, were charming and eccentric, Aligre were pushing the needle towards 'weird'. They had an act involving trained rats! Our kids loved the Aligre guys and snuck in to the tent every evening to watch their show. At their matinee that I saw on my day off, there was only a smattering of people in the audience. A few turkeys made up the numbers, sitting on the back-row benches near the roof of the tent where they watched the show in silence, punctuated only by the odd bout of irritated preening. Another act brought on a young black bull with dangerous looking horns that careered around the tiny circus ring until, without warning, it took a sharp left, jumped clean out of the ring and found itself flailing and thrashing its legs in the front-row seats, scattering shocked onlookers as if a bomb were about to go off. From the relative safety of six rows back, I got up and sauntered away while the Aligre guys attempted to calm the bull and remove it without getting themselves gored.

As fellow travelling-show people, we tended to like them automatically. Yes, they were mad, but you had to admire their skills and bravado, so we generally looked out for each other, especially as we had a spate of bicycle thefts in Barcelona. Several cherished classic Amsterdam sit-up-and-beg bikes with reverse pedal brakes were gone. A few days later, on a bus ride across the city with John Kilby, Brillo was taken by an opportunist. Poor John didn't realise until it was too late, and a search proved hopeless. When he got back to camp he was clearly devastated by the loss of his best friend, and sadly we never saw Brillo again. After that, the two remaining border collies, Ufo and Jig, were closely watched.

MORE POSITIVELY, THE THEATRE SHOWS were the hit events of the festival, and rave reviews in the Catalan newspapers brought in throngs of enthusiastic audiences. The bin men went back to work at 5.00 a.m. one morning, and the sun shone. Wandering around the side-streets away from the Ramblas I stumbled across an old shoemaker's shop window that displayed a beautiful pair of tan shoes, similar in design to a desert boot, and at such a reasonable price I couldn't resist.

When I got back wearing the new shoes, everyone wanted a pair. From then on I began to enjoy Spain. Barcelona's attractions, like the semi-constructed Cathedral and Gaudi's other architectural delights, plus the magic fountain at Montjuic with seven billion possible light and water jet displays – not bad for something built in 1929 – made that September an enlightening and inspirational time.

Theatre on the Beach

Come October we moved south to Sitges and set up on the beach. The three shows we were performing – the tragicomic *Arthur*, Shakespeare's *Hamlet* and *Tall Stories* based on the García Márquez short story, 'A Very Old Man with Enormous Wings' – were perfect fare and easy to promote. Happy days.

Arthur was classic early Footsbarn material, very much an adaptation for the stage with an audience at close quarters, not unlike Monty Python's *Holy Grail* movie with its irreverent humour and ladled with silliness and seriousness in equal measure. It was a perfect companion show to *Hamlet* which was a much more mature theatre piece. The actors clearly relished performing *Arthur* but there had been a discussion about when we were going to drop it from the repertoire after a two-year run. It was settled by fate when a tremendous overnight storm flooded the tent, destroyed the costumes and basically left *Arthur* going down in a lake. I was sad about that, as it was a favourite show and I never tired of watching and helping the actors from the wings. It was full of uproarious humour, including a chaotic scene that abruptly concluded when a woman came running and screaming round the front of the stage and suddenly had her head removed with one clean swipe of a knight's sword. The severed head nearly always landed in the lap of a shocked audience member, whose horror-stricken face had the rest of the audience in hysterics until he or she realised it was a dummy head with red ribbons streaming

'Barber' Petal shaving Joao on the beach

from the neck. The final scene was terrifying, with the two knights, played by Rod and Paddy, wearing chainmail armour, whole head and face helmets and enormous platform boots so they towered above everyone, fighting to the death with giant clanking swords. In tandem with Simon's deafening percussion effects with drums and cymbals at his mercy, it always left the audience awestruck. These were the scenes we created after darkness fell, when only the lapping of the sea could be heard outside.

In complete contrast, our daytime lives were relaxed and fun; we were right on the beach in Sitges, with a bit of warmth still in the October sunshine. There was a tap at a stand pipe for our use, though the water that came out of it was salt water, so it wasn't for drinking, but I did use it to mix glue for sticking up posters around the town. The glue went all lumpy in the bucket, so I got stuck in with my hands, squeezing out the lumps. When I wiped my hands, the skin started coming away in ribbons as if it was a ghastly horror movie. I was terrified. I imagined my hands were going to melt down to bare bones. It was one of those awful nightmare moments when you find yourself in a new country with an unfamiliar language. I wondered if I'd asked for the wrong thing when I bought the glue and had been given sulphuric acid. Thankfully, the pharmacist who had sold the glue sorted me out with bandages, gloves and medication.

Around this time, I started driving The Brute. I told Warwick, who usually drove it, that I'd need a body like his to drive that thing. He said, 'This *is* a bodybuilding course. Get in!' I spent an hour in Barcelona traffic trying to find the right gears in an old-fashioned crash box and to master the method of double clutching in the hope that the horrible noise from grinding gear teeth would wane in time. Slowly but surely I did get the hang of it, but not before my own grinding teeth had given me the worst headache I could ever remember.

Fortunately, things got better as I went on ahead of the company to set up a gig in Xàtiva and began to enjoy the whole weird adventure. For the first time in my life, I felt 'out there' beyond the comfort zone of my previous life experiences and was thrilled by the sights, smells, sounds and tastes I was confronted with. I'd had my share of cool experiences in my short life, but somehow this was *real* adventuring. I remember feeling resentful of the British tourists who were landing at local airports for their Spanish holidays. Harbouring a totally unreasonable attitude which amounted to raw inverted snobbery, I thought, 'Tourists! Tuh! What do they know?' *We* had crawled our way across Europe, steeping ourselves in the sublime exotica of European culture. We were the toast of Amsterdam and Freiburg, sponsored by the British Council. We were the darlings of the French national press in Avignon. We were on fire in Catalonia and Andalusia, bringing a bombastic breath of fresh energy to stuffy international theatre. But here's the question: Were we really all this, or were we just a bunch of hippies on the road with a cheap circus? Because within a few months we had thrown all that momentum down the tubes with a chaotic, stumbling tour of Portugal.

IF THE REALITY OF KEEPING THIS SHOW on the road was always going to be challenging, at this point in time it was impossible to foresee that within a year we'd be down and out in Jerez de la Frontera. For now, the delights of Spain in benign autumn weather and the brilliant reaction to the shows we performed kept our spirits high. For me, reaching Moorish towns that began with the letter X was a new experience, along with eating the fruit of the cactus, the orangey-red prickly pear – which really is edible – only to discover to my cost that I would spend days trying to pick the tiniest pesky needles out of my hands.

We avoided the sprawling coastal resorts and drove down the inland country roads to Yecla, taking the scenic route to Granada and passing the strange but friendly troglodytes and their caves dotted across the sloping hillside at Guadix. It was November already, and the low-angled sun combined with the breeze to make the yellowing birch leaves shimmer like gold coins dancing against the blue sky. The landscape looked more like the wild west as narrow orange groves in Valencia were replaced by vast open plains.

At one point I drove past two gypsy girls, miles from anywhere, walking along the side of the dusty road. As The Brute got close to them, making its usual roaring six-cylinder noises, the elder girl turned towards me and, shielding her sister with her arm, took a step back off the road and looked up. But it wasn't just a look she gave me: it was a black-eyed barrelling stare, so intense it went through me and sent a shudder deep down into some lower region I never knew I had. No one across the whole Iberian peninsula would look at me again with such piercing intensity as this poor, weather-beaten teenager, and its fleeting nature made it all the more elusively seductive.

Whenever I try to recall this tiny incident, I remember the feeling that accompanied me for the rest of that day, like a bell that tolled deep in my belly because someone had seen into my soul and I'd been exposed. I decided that this girl, in that time-stopping moment, expressed something beyond sexuality or passion and embodied a raw humanity and the very nature of Spain. I didn't come across anything quite like it for years to come, until one day in 1985 I saw an image of an Afghan girl on the cover of *National Geographic* magazine. Steve McCurry's famous photograph of a refugee called Sharbat Gula in Pakistan was the closest thing to that Spanish gypsy stare I got that day in 1981, except that my girl's eyes were black!

As an introduction to Moorish architectural heritage and design, the Alhambra palace in Granada is as good as it gets. It was once recorded that upon entering Granada, Francisco Asís de Icaza met a beggar on the street and turned to his aide, saying, 'Give him alms, woman, for there is nothing worse than being blind in Granada.'

In places like this where the sun's heat is punishing, the sight and sound of running water is almost sacred. Here at the palace, water is given a central role, following an open channel down the centre aisle of the building and out into the courtyard, where lions spout the very source of life. Inspired and awestruck as I was by the splendour and decorative abundance of the whole palace, I couldn't help falling

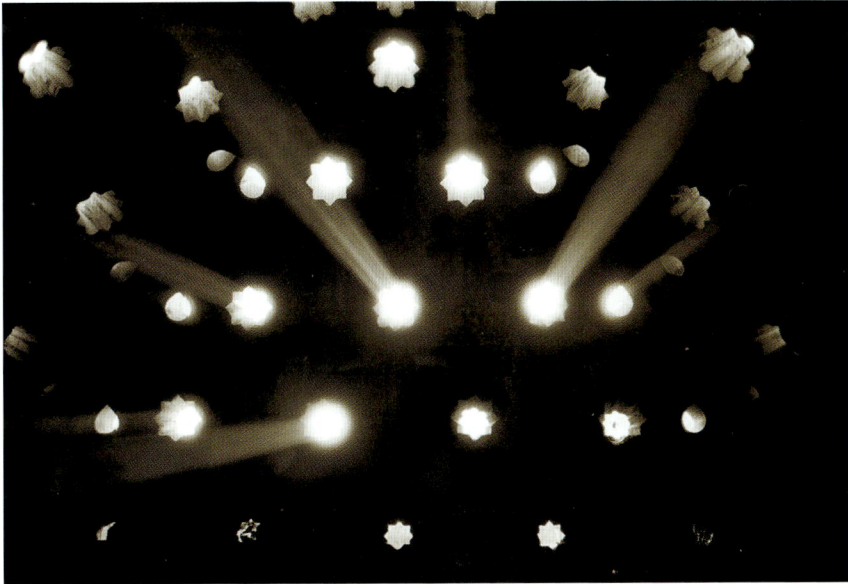

Alhambra Palace bathroom, Granada

in love with the tiny bath house, built without windows to retain a cave-like coolness, its domed ceiling punched with star-shaped holes allowing shafts of sunlight to scatter stars across the floor tiles. I wanted to take the idea home and build one myself.

Granada's university campus where we set up the tent and performed to mostly students was another successful gig, marred only by the disappearance of a brand new canvas banner that Charmian had made and I had spent several days painting with 'Footsbarn Theatre' emblazoned across it. Hung high across the street at the approach to the theatre tent, it had obviously been stolen in the night with the intention of decorating some student's flat, and that was the end of that.

More positively, the students really loved the show we were doing, *The Very Old Man With Enormous Wings*. The sickly and decrepit old man speaking a strange language and deporting shabby wings who had landed in the back yard of a local peasant was brilliantly played by Joe, even though he didn't have an intelligible word to speak through the whole play. His plaintive song still haunts me, the one he sang before taking off and disappearing at the end. Before that took place the peasant and his family tried to take advantage of his fall from the heavens by putting him in a pen and charging the public a fee for a glimpse of the 'angel', with hilarious results. It was another of Footsbarn's exquisite stage adaptations using music and buffoonery while the story still managed to carry a cautionary moral punch.

I travelled a lot in convoy with Joe, who always drove the Magirus Deutz truck. Joe was a brilliant open-air cook. He had the happy knack of being able to set up a camp by the roadside in a carefully chosen secluded spot and within minutes have a fire going for barbecued chicken or gambas – delicious, plump, Spanish tiger prawns. I was fortunate to belong to what became the 'Boys' Club' – single guys who cooked for each other – and both Joe and Bruno were excellent cooks. My own efforts to wrestle with the art tended to result in a right gallimaufry of the ingredients available. But Joe and Bruno never complained.

The simplicity of those days fostered an appreciation of life's great pleasures. One evening, after a day's hard driving along the old Ruta de los Pueblos Blancos, we sat drinking wine around the campfire and watched a deep red sun slip silently into the dusty horizon, while on the opposite horizon, back over the mountain tops from where we had come, a fat full moon the colour of orange marmalade crept into a mauve sky. I wondered if I had any film in the camera and, if I did, would it capture this low-light scene with any coherent definition. Unlike modern digital cameras and phones, in those days film cameras struggled in near-dark situations. I decided to commit the scene to memory instead. In what seemed like a few short minutes the moon had already turned a flaky white and was flying high in a black night sky, and so, without a breath of wind to disturb the inebriated atmosphere, all was right with the world.

Of course, all was *not* right with the world, because when we reached Seville the following day it stank like a shit-house and the river had no water in it. In the converted church that served as our theatre we were told there was a toilet here somewhere but it could only be flushed once a day. Once a day! There were fifteen of us working there. It felt like the whole tour was reaching an overbaked and tiresome end. In fairness to Seville, it had its moments of magic, the shows were full and the old town was a gem. But we were eager to get to the winter base camp in Portugal and do the final shows of the year in Odemira before resting up for Christmas. There we could savour the prospect of creating a new show. I recently found the newsletter that I wrote for the company that Christmas. Here's an extract from the final paragraph:

> *We celebrated the completion of the circle (around Europe) with the last gig of the tour in Odemira, just twenty miles away from where it had been created back in January. The children, for their part of the celebration, were in exuberant form as the 'Footlets', performing their own version of the Circus Tosov. After half an hour of bubble and squeak hilarity, the adults, amazed and kidwinked, happily*

soothed their aching ribs and considered retirement. And it was a celebration, and it felt good. The sparks from the fire lost themselves in a spangled sky where shooting stars, like burning ideas, kindled thoughts of a new show in our minds.

How romantic!

Portugal, a Base Camp and a New Show, 1981–82

Although I'd been hearing all about the base camp at Baranco in Portugal's Alentejo province and how it had been set up the previous year, as a new boy, only joining up in the summer, I'd never seen it in person. In fact, I'd never been to Portugal at all. On this occasion, I travelled from Seville as a passenger with Henry in his truck, happy to watch the landscape change from Estremadura's arid wasteland, where Spain ran out of land, to the Algarve's relative freshness. As soon as we crossed the border it seemed that the flies stopped bothering us. I was going to enjoy Portugal, and I didn't throw up – which had to be a good sign because we were going to get stuck here for nearly a year. Happily and unhappily, we were going to be rich in the generous hospitality of the Portuguese people, but we were also going to be desperately poor and woefully lacking in investment and support. On my first day trucking across the Algarve, Henry extolled the virtues of life in Portugal: the food, the music, the temperament – all so different to Spain.

Turning north towards Serra de Monchique, we left the tourist strip behind and climbed into the mountains until it was time to stop for lunch. I asked Henry if I could borrow his racing bike, head up the mountain and meet him further along the road. As I raced ahead in tee shirt and shorts, I didn't take account of the speed I'd be going once past the summit at Monchique. I was flying down in zigzag fashion at speeds in excess of what the truck could match on

Rod hitches a ride during an Easter parade in Lagos, Algarve

the switchback road. The temperature dropped sharply on the north side of the mountains, and as it was late November the sun dropped like a stone just after five o'clock. I realised I had no lights, no wallet, no money, no identification, no warm clothes and not a word of Portuguese! Henry had got to the summit and, thinking he must have passed me, turned around and went back. Freezing and scared out of my wits, I was never so glad to see the lights of the old Leyland truck when Henry eventually crept down the twisting road as I pushed the bike and my exhausted body back up the mountain several hours later. It was a lesson I should have paid more attention to because I would do something similar again in twelve months' time.

Having families with lots of children on the road made Footsbarn completely different to most other touring theatres. In fact, one could argue that amid the group of mad musicians, actors and artists that formed the company, the children were the sane ones. Given the extraordinary circumstances of their lifestyle, it is a testament to their resilience that most of these children have grown into fine adult specimens with normal families of their own.

Sometimes, when we were doing shows in France, I took my turn to make breakfast for the kids and would go off to the supermarket with them to get supplies.

'What's your favourite thing?' I'd ask.

'Sweaty piss!' they shouted in unison.

Sweaty piss? It took me a while to realise it was their pet name for Petit Suisse, their favourite yogurt. It was a good enough joke to make me laugh out loud.

AS WE SET UP CAMP FOR THE WINTER months at Baranco, just a couple of miles inland from the coast in the eucalyptus forest, two things lifted my spirits completely: the colour of the sea at Milfontes, a true aquamarine blue, and the blissfully hot showers at the public baths in Odemira. Scales fell from my eyes and skin so that, for the first time in many months, I felt refreshed in body and spirit. I also found a way of venting frustrations on winter days when the clouds rolled in and the wind got up. I would ride down to the beach at Almograve and shout and roar at the ocean waves, hurling the pent-up tension into the all-consuming sea.

Baranco de Cima, to give it its full name, was a wide, hill-top opening in the forest with several dishevelled old single-storey farm buildings that could be used for kitchen and communal areas and for rehearsals. The eucalyptus trees ran down the valleys and covered the next hills, and the next, as far as the eye could see.

At Baranco most people had their places, reclaiming spots where they had parked or pitched tents the previous winter. I found the walled garden down the hill to my liking, so I pitched my tent in the gardener's shed because there was no roof on it. Here, the well, which was the only source of water for the whole camp, was easily accessible, so I didn't have to carry great plastic tanks of water up the hill like all the others.

At daybreak the kids were first to arrive. Usually it was Rebecca, Corinna and maybe Daisy, all eager to wake me up and make tea for me as soon as I got a fire going. The fire consisted of a handful of dry eucalyptus leaves and twigs, which was enough to boil the kettle. Unlike in Ireland, where you could spend all day trying to light a fire outdoors in February, here in Alentejo you could set fire to the entire region with a careless match. The only trouble was that the children had very little patience and kept asking if the kettle was boiling. The tea ended up milky, tepid and thin. If the kids had bigger fish to fry – if there was some other poor bachelor to drag out of his sleeping bag up the hill – they would disappear in a giggling flash, and peace would descend once more. That is, until the young Portuguese women arrived at the well to wash and usually ran around naked to dry off, throwing soaking tee shirts and bars of soap at each other.

One morning, arriving at the top of the hill to see what everyone was up to and to check in on the rehearsals, I found Rod hammering something into the ground with the heel of his boot, cursing with every blow. It turned out he'd been stung by a scorpion when he put his boots on. Okay, lesson learned. Don't leave your boots lying on their side on the ground overnight.

In the night, the farmer's huge sow would announce her arrival by banging on the wooden door in the garden wall, which I always latched before turning in, no matter how inebriated I was. Mother pig left her *banbhs* asleep and played a nightly game that became a ritual. She banged the door with her ample flanks until it gave way, and then she'd trot round the garden pulling up whatever vegetable took her fancy. Meanwhile, having heard the sound of the door giving way, I would haul myself out of bed naked in pursuit and join in the ritual.

We were two pink creatures dancing in the moonlight, one squealing with delight, the other cursing and throwing sods until the one with four legs tired of the game and disappeared through the door. Pretending to have gotten the better of the pig, I began to enjoy the game after a few nights and admired her for her brazen and enterprising excursions, all in search of a decent midnight snack. Then I remembered that old phrase, 'dogs look up to you, cats look down on you and pigs are equal', and I wondered who was fooling who.

When I returned to bed, the heavy scent of mimosa blossom that hung over the little shed sent me back to sleep until the wind got up, stirring the giant metal windmill that towered over the well. This set off a round of rusty whining noises that would have scared the dead, sounding like a cross between chalk scratched across a blackboard and a train screeching to a halt.

ON THE WHOLE, THE TIME AT BARANCO was a happy and creative experience. There were a few partner rearrangements causing heartaches for some, meaning that some fell in love and others suffered the fallout. That's life, I suppose. We had the company of two Portuguese helpers, Paulo and Joao M, whose cheery faces were always uplifting. When asked how he was, Joao would always say, 'Oh, I'm completely happy, absolutely happy.' For a big man, he was a real twinkle toes, and watching him dance at the local dance halls where we played live music was always a treat.

After one of these lively dances, I was returning to camp with Paolo as dawn broke, after we had piled all the speakers, amps and instruments into the back of what I called the 'refugee truck'. It was one of the many old Leyland trucks we had on the road, only this one had a bare-bones interior with just two bench seats, so it also served as basic transport when we needed to go across the border to Spain, turn around and get the passport stamped and the visa renewed for another three months. It was then that you *felt* like a refugee.

Paolo was driving and was chatting away to me, the only passenger aboard, as the truck pitched and tossed over the dried-up potholes along the sandy track. All of a sudden we were heading straight for a eucalyptus tree. 'Paolo!' Too late! He was fast asleep, chin on chest. The tremendous jolt as the truck slammed into the tree woke him up and no great damage was done to the tree or the truck, which had only a ding in the bumper, so his imploring demands not to tell anyone back at camp were easy enough to agree to. Don't worry, Paolo, your secret is safe with me.

I knew that sandy track like the back of my hand because Alison and I would go the market in Cercal in the same truck at least once a week to get provisions for the great task of feeding the five thousand. Well, it was only sixty in reality, but it was double what the company usually had on tour because so many friends had turned up to help with the new show. The Portuguese women at the market always managed to secretly stuff extra food, vegetables and treats into the top of each sack, so that unloading the goods in the kitchen always came with surprises, no matter how closely we'd watched things being loaded at the market.

The chicken that was roasted spatchcock-style at the open-air market in Vila Nova de Milfontes tasted so intensely chickeny that it took me right back to my childhood in Anglesey, probably because the birds had been running around the garden the previous day. But I suspected that it was something else too. It was straightforward country fare, way before standardisation, supermarket classification and future health and safety requirements so that, especially in this part of humble Portugal, you were witnessing a way of life and husbandry that was likely to disappear in the years to come. It was a phenomenon we sometimes stumbled upon by accident – in the mountains of France or Italy, for example, when travelling off the beaten track, a piece of beef or pork bought from a small village butcher was so utterly melt-in-the-mouth delicious the experience would stay with you for the rest of your life.

I started taking minutes at meetings because no one seemed to have a record of what decisions had been made and what actions agreed upon. It was suggested that the process had been somewhat organic, but I didn't have much time for that, fine though it sounded. So I continued to make notes so that we could refer back to decisions we'd made without argument, and I think everyone appreciated it after a while (though I could never be quite sure). If Alison sat beside me she would try to put me off by whispering, 'Don't listen to this rubbish, it won't make any difference.' And then I'd find it difficult to concentrate.

The Devil, The Doctor and The Fool

It was at Baranco where the actors set to work devising the new show and by February they had started rehearsing in the old farm building. Called *The Devil, The Doctor and The Fool*, the show was based on a mumming play about the cycle of the seasons, with each season personified, along with help from other characters representing death and rebirth. It was acted out through music and mime with a minimum of spoken language, so it would be a suitable show to tour in any country, but especially in rural Portugal and Spain. Gregg, Jon B and Simon did a wonderful job creating the music.

Sketches for the Ribboner and the Doctor

Poster for The Devil, The Doctor and The Fool

One or two characters from the show went on to enjoy a longer life due to the ease with which they transferred to the street acts and parades in future years. Death on stilts was one of the best. Although the show was well received everywhere it was performed, it had a relatively short life and, for reasons that will become clear, we had to abandon it before the year was out. At this point we were still entertaining notions of touring in Brazil, or at least making it to Rio. God knows how because it was doubtful that we would get invited, but that was the ambition.

The poster design for the show had to be simple enough to be screen-printed in two passes and colourful enough to be attractive and stand out. With primitive equipment, I managed to paint a lightfast image directly onto a large sheet of acetate film using photographer's 'liquid opaque', which was like painting with sloppy mud. It worked well, and I was able to follow my drawn-out design on paper, simply by laying the acetate on top, making a kind of window, and tracing what I could see through it onto the surface.

Finishing before lunch, I left it to dry in the spring sunshine and went off up the hill for a bite to eat. Returning an hour later to see if it was dry and ready for the next stage, I found to my horror it had dried too quickly and cracked like a dried-up river bed. Hmm, wait a minute. This is really cool. The image now had an antique looking crazed effect made by what artists tend to call a happy accident. Sure enough, the printed poster had a maze of tiny cracks like a potter's crackle glaze, and it did lend a certain aged quality to the finished article. Hundreds and hundreds of posters were printed by hand on that tour, ably assisted by the kids who spread the wet posters along the seats in the tent to dry.

The local people were curious and very friendly. We witnessed the nearby village of Brunheiras getting electricity for the first time, and the day it was switched on the celebrations continued all through the night. They were still going on when I arrived at the little taverna at nine o'clock the next morning. The local guys were fond of their mopeds; typically, the smaller the engine the louder the noise. I heard one in the distance as I was about to buy cigarettes. There was something about this guy's progress over the bumpy dirt road, with his comical pudding-bowl helmet and huge strap under the chin, that stopped me in my tracks.

Approaching the front door at alarming speed, his engine cut out, bringing him silently rolling by right in front of me. He sailed on for a few metres, stopped, quivered slightly, then keeled over sideways and lay in a heap, snoring. The taverna keeper and I looked at each other. 'He is all right already,' was his verdict, so we laughed and left him to sleep it off in the winter sunshine.

I preferred the lovely white light and soft hissing sound from the Tilley lamps that most of us had. They ran on paraffin and had to be primed before lighting the gauze with a match. Some things had to be suffered or tolerated, like UHT milk, which was awful. It was impossible to find fresh milk or a decent marmalade. Help sometimes arrived with visiting friends in the form of Barry's tea or Marmite. But there were plenty of pluses too. The Portuguese like their gadgets, so their hardware stores and bric-a-brac shops were a trove of wonderful things. Workshop and kitchen knives were perfectly weighted and beautifully crafted. Facecloth-covered sponges, perfect for a body wash when showers and baths were unavailable, which was most of the time, made daily life more bearable. Good-quality toilet paper was highly prized and coveted. Travelling anywhere in southern Europe – especially in France, where their toilets were still the squat type – if you didn't bring your own supplies you would be left staring at an empty roll holder on the wall.

Being in one place for several months encouraged all kinds of innovative projects for living on the road. Caravan stoves were made from converted gas bottles, while huge, black, plastic tanks balanced on top of a truck or bus and rigged with a Heath Robinson-type of pipe work would deliver a decent shower of hot water heated by the sun.

The local shepherds were great fun. They often joined us at night-time, playing music and singing folk songs from the Alentejo region. I loved their sheepskin jackets made with a short open front, shaped like a waistcoat and a long back like a tailcoat: perfect for standing or sitting in front of the fire with your back to the cold night air. You could tell when they were coming from the sound of the goat bells tinkling and clunking across the valley. 'Bom dia!' they would bellow as if you were hard of hearing, then stand there beaming, squinting and wheezing through missing teeth. One of the younger guys was brilliant on the accordion, so sometimes the entire camp was lost in music under the stars. Nearly everyone in Footsbarn could play at least one instrument, and everyone loved to sing, so many Portuguese folk songs were added to the repertoire. I wonder now what happened to the shepherds. Maybe it's a way of life that has disappeared.

On Christmas Day, I walked through the orange groves so I could taste the fruit straight from the tree. I was so ignorant of the way citrus fruit was cultivated, I was amazed that an orange from one tree could taste completely different from the fruit of another tree in the same grove. I'd never thought much about it. An orange was always just an orange. My wife would be ashamed to hear me admitting this, since she grew up in Los Angeles with orange and lemon trees in the back yard, but for me, back then, it was an innocent revelation, and I decided that oranges were royalty among fruit, amazingly protected from the searing heat by their oily zest and woolly pith. As a colour, orange is still just orange. I mean, you don't hear of light orange or dark orange or variations as you do with yellow, like mustard or primrose. Maybe 'burnt' orange, but most of the time orange is just orange.

Gregg with the A flat horn

Daniel, who owned the land we camped on, made a welcome party by offering a pig. Portuguese women arrived from somewhere as the sound of mopeds came through the forest like giant gnats. It was suddenly a hive of activity with trestle tables in preparation for the butchery. It was all so busy that nobody noticed Daisy, only six at the time, standing there watching as the pig, squealing for its life, had its throat cut. Daisy started laughing. Not a normal laugh, but something gathering up into hysterics until the pig's

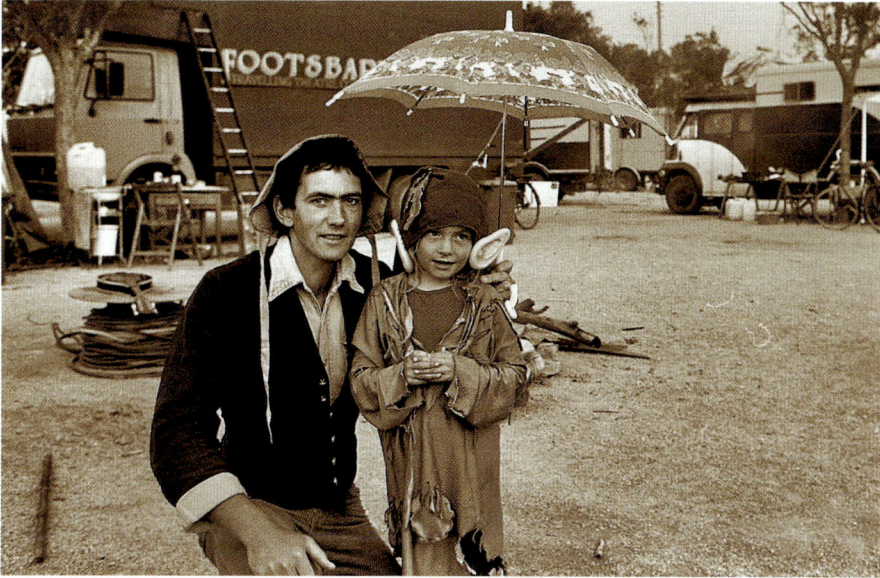

Ted with Daisy, Setúbal, Portugal

protests faded into a gurgle as the animal bled out. It was only then, as Daisy's inane laughter filled the void, that she was noticed and quickly ushered away and comforted. I felt more sorry for Daisy than for the pig. The pig's demise was just life on the farm, and we gave our thanks to Daniel and to the pig for its sacrifice. For Daisy, it was a lesson learned but a shocking one.

On the Road Again

The tour of Portugal didn't start well for me. There was nothing wrong with the new show – everyone seemed to like it, and it was 'running in' nicely, with tweaks here and there. No, the problem was a personal one. As morning broke after a performance in a hill-top village north of Faro in the Algarve, I reeled out of my bed in the cab of the truck, doubled up, retching and gasping in pain as if some-one had just hit me in the balls with a sledgehammer. I was packed off to hospital in Beja, where the diagnosis of a simple streptococcal infection was sorted out pretty quickly, thank God, with antibiotics.

The doctors were more concerned about a lump the size of an egg in my neck, clearly visible just above the collarbone. Not that I'd noticed – I couldn't remember the last time I'd studied myself in a decent mirror.

The doctors said I would have to go to Lisbon for tests when I felt better. They were worried I might have goitre, which was common enough in Portugal, where there was a lack of iodine in the water. All this deflected attention from the original ailment, the attack in the 'Balkans'. They dismissed it, saying that the squalid lifestyle we led, swimming in rivers and such, was probably to blame. What I didn't realise, and would not discover until ten years later and I was already married, was that from that fateful day in the Algarve and for the rest of my life, I was sterile!

Once the tour got into its stride, we realised it was going to be arduous. We had lots of really good times; we ate and drank well and enjoyed the Portuguese people and their culture. But we never

Alison, Frey and Phil – No matter how little money we had
there was always cake for a birthday

seemed to gain attention to the same degree we had in other countries. Community councils were enthusiastic but wrung their hands in pity because they had so little money and not much at all to spend on a foreign theatre company that rattled around Portugal without an official invitation. The British Council dropped us because we had fallen off their strategic map. It had only been seven years since the quiet revolution in Portugal in 1974, and the councils were still trying to sort things out. Some of the more open and generous councils in Alentejo were communist.

Sitting at a cafe one lunchtime in Setúbal after putting up posters around town, I saw a businessman approach and sit at a table next to mine. He was neatly dressed in the city style: dark suit, white shirt, nice tie and polished shoes. Out of a smart-looking briefcase he pulled a clear plastic bag full of fresh sardines. He handed the bag to the cafe proprietor, who graciously took them inside, grilled them and brought them back out on a plate. Then the businessman tucked in with bread and white wine. Now, I don't wish to insult the humble sardine. They are often barbecued on the beach here in Portugal, and they are delicious, but it seemed to say a lot. If this was how a businessman lived, we were going to need a miracle to feed a huge travelling company with over thirty people, and a few loaves and fishes might be all we could expect. So if we were going to be poor, we might as well enjoy the sunshine and get on with it. Sometimes the actors and musicians went out busking in the streets simply to provide breakfast for the kids the following morning.

It was about this time that a very pregnant Laura got herself into a local hospital when the labour pains told her that her first child was about to be born to herself and Jamie. I'd had a couple of run-ins with Jamie over the months on the road, one of which nearly came to blows after he got himself in a rage over God knows what and accused me of being a pseudo-Irish fake full of pretence. I was just a useless Sassenach! Before he tried to hit me, I decided to remove my front two false teeth, which were on a plate in those days, because

I wasn't going to risk getting the expensive little buggers broken. When I grinned at him he laughed so hard that we fell into a heap and dragged ourselves off to the bar to drink the blues away.

Seriously, though, it was a near miss – Jamie had a darkly *frampold* temper as well as a fun, high-spirited nature. We all had our tantrums and quarrels from time to time, and Jamie and Laura certainly had theirs, but thankfully Laura could hold her own and match him. They both had so much to like about them, and if Jamie's Scottish feistiness was a handful, we owed him a debt of gratitude for keeping our trucks, buses and caravans safely maintained and roadworthy.

A few of us were in the cafe playing pool and drinking coffee the day after Laura went into labour in the local hospital. Suddenly Jamie was there at the door of the cafe, appearing in silhouette against the bright light of the sun glaring behind him in the open street. He stood in the doorway trembling, unable to move, and looked at us all. And then his face screwed up and tears streamed down. Oh no, Jamie, surely not! Oh no! Eventually the voice broke from his gaping mouth: 'I'm a dad,' he blurted out. And then we all grabbed him and cheered

Publicity photo for The Devil, The Doctor and The Fool *show, Cascais*

and brought him inside, where we sat him down and had a drink to celebrate the new arrival. His weary body stopped convulsing and he smiled through the tears. Laura and baby Neil were both fine.

After Setúbal I took the truck the long way round to Lisbon on the coast road via the pretty fishing village of Sesimbra. I stopped for the night on the edge of a clifftop with a fabulous view of the Atlantic Ocean to wake up to. Greeted by a gorgeous bright April morning, I was squinting and yawning, trying to look out to sea, when I became aware of a deep thrumming sound, the kind that you could feel through your body. Then there were voices, speaking English! And suddenly a naval ship flying the Canadian flag sliced my view in half. It was so close I could have landed a stone on it, as I was at least thirty or forty feet above the ship as it passed by.

It was a wake-up call in more ways than one. A newspaper I picked up in the city that day revealed rumours that a crisis was looming in the Falkland Islands and that several Commonwealth navy vessels had been on alert, though their governments weren't sure what to do. It soon became clear what Margaret Thatcher was going to do, and here we were touring in Portugal and Spain, where they referred to the islands as the Malvinas. Even though we had an international group of personnel, the company was still viewed as British. What would the Latin countries do now that Maggie's army and navy were on the way to give the Argies a good bashing, as some British tabloids put it with their usual jingoistic relish?

Cascais, the fashionable Lisbon resort town north of the city, should have offered us rich pickings, but hardly anyone came. *Raiders of the Lost Ark* seemed to be more attractive fare, and most of us went to see it at the cinema before our two-week stay was over. We made use of this quiet time to paint all the trucks in a uniform company livery of maroon and cream – all except for The Brute, which remained in bright yellow for some reason, but even that got a fresh coat of paint and new sign writing. I took a photograph of the actors and musicians in front of the truck when it was ready, and it remains a reminder of the exuberance and brimming health and youth of that group. It was often used in publicity even though Gregg was missing from the picture.

We were well received in Lisbon and at long last got some good notices in the national press. Luckily, too, the bizarre behaviour of the Argentinian junta had been deemed to be dubious and unwise in many Latin countries, and even among the Argentinian people themselves. It could have been so much worse. Not that many of us, if any at all, backed Margaret Thatcher, and I remember on several occasions after the show finished, Rod would bid farewell to the audience with the old adage, 'Make love, not war!' before the actors bowed out.

America, July 1982

F lying into Denver, the mile-high city on the edge of the Rockies, took us out of poverty and gave us a taste of efficiency that comes with the American let's-do-it attitude to everything. The World Theater Festival technician assigned to us was a confident and assertive young woman who arrived bristling with tools attached to a belt around the hips. I introduced her to our own technicians, Dave and Johnny. The look on their faces was priceless, while their Adam's apples simultaneously took the lift to the first floor and back down again. Over the week or so we were there, I think she made a favourable impression, especially as our guys were so often given responses like, 'No, we can't get that' during set-ups at festivals across Europe. Here in Denver she would say, 'Yes, I can get that, but maybe what you really need is this.' And she'd come up with some novel way of solving the problem.

The journalists were only too glad to publish whatever story you wanted them to write. The modern pod-shaped tent we were given was perched on a concrete plaza in front of one of the main theatre buildings. Directly underneath this vast concrete slab was a

Randy and Mick (on the left) and Pat Bracken from Galway (in red) join us in Colorado for the American visit

four-lane underpass where huge American cars wallowed and lunged around the place at all hours of the day and night. The audiences were thrilled with the show, and it was all very enjoyable. I was able to buy whatever materials I needed for printing posters without much fuss, often all at the same shopping complex or business park. Most of all, I didn't have to get official stamps from the tobacconist and go to the municipal offices to get permission to blow my nose, and shops didn't close for siesta.

Philippe Petit was there doing his tightrope act and street performances. Yes, the same guy who walked a wire between the Twin Towers of the World Trade Center in New York. He came in for a lot of stick when he took his baby with him on the high-wire act here in Denver, but he sure got the publicity he was looking for.

A kind invitation to visit a commune so that we could water the horses, so to speak, in the hills of southern Colorado on the way to Santa Fe in New Mexico was enlightening for the way they were almost self-sufficient in energy and food. If you don't automatically think of Americans as being kind, generous and hospitable, then I would urge you to think again, because in my experience they're right up there with the best. We were treated royally during our five-week stay, and if some of the group felt awkward working in such a wealthy environment, and criticised the blandness of midwest culture and its architecture and all-too-evident excesses, waste accumulation and obesity, I felt it would have been churlish in the extreme to hurl that in our hosts' faces, and thankfully no one did.

After setting up right beside the Santa Fe Festival Theatre, we spent a week doing shows in a specially made outdoor arena during the balmy August evenings after darkness fell. It was just what the doctor ordered. All *The Devil, The Doctor and The Fool* shows we performed there were sold out and rapturously received. It seemed a shame to have to leave. The southwestern landscapes and colours of New Mexico, the silver and turquoise arts and crafts, the adobe houses and cowboy-and-Indian culture, along with the clothes, boots and spurs that went with it, seemed to appeal to the Footsbarn way of life more readily than American city life did.

Madeline Kahn was starring in the Santa Fe Festival Theatre's own production of *Blithe Spirit* right there and then, inside on the main stage. She was quite a catch for the theatre because she was still riding high on the success of several films by Mel Brooks, like *Blazing Saddles* and *Young Frankenstein*. The diminutive actress was mobbed when she came to see our show.

Many years later I was told that a poster of mine had sold for two thousand dollars in Santa Fe. I said, 'No, that's a mistake, maybe it was two hundred.' But the figure was right. The story was that the Santa Fe Festival Theatre in the 1980s had been run by an administration with a large number of gay men. They were devastated by the AIDS virus at the end of the decade, and one of my posters happened to be in the fundraising auction to help the sufferers. Hence the hefty sum.

A Day in Manhattan

Flying out of Albuquerque, we had a stopover of about six hours in New York before the onward flight back to Europe. Accompanied by Simon, the percussionist with the group, we headed into Manhattan from JFK Airport with hardly a cent in our pockets. I managed to sell my father's gold signet ring, which I'd been carrying around for years but never wore, to a Polish jeweller in Greenwich Village. It gave us enough money for lunch, a whizz round town, the fares back to the airport and a bit to spare.

'Have you ever seen the Chrysler Building?' I asked Simon over lunch.

'What's that?' he said, more interested in the sandwich in front of him.

'We'll go and see it after lunch,' I said, thinking back to the summer job I had three years earlier when I used to stare at this building from my desk at the *Art & Antiques* magazine office twenty-nine floors up on Madison Avenue.

Simply getting to the Chrysler Building was an adventure. The Rastafarian taxi driver was so stoned, he mixed up the numbers of the streets with the avenues, so it took a while to get him pointing in the right direction, although I suspected he was doing it on purpose. 'Oh, right, yeah, man, of course.' Eventually getting out at 42nd Street, we craned our necks to look skyward, like all tourists do, to see the majestic Chrysler Building towering to infinity with its silver spire glinting in the sunlight. But wait, what's that? It looked like a tiny scaffold around the base of the spire. It was difficult to tell. Crossing the street, we headed for the front doors. Inside the foyer we were greeted with gorgeous art deco designs, exquisite marble walls and painted murals, typical of the pre-Depression opulence and exuberance of 1930s New World architecture.

We hardly had time to take in all the paintings when an elevator door opened just beside us, revealing yet more sumptuous design work. It seemed so inviting it was a shame to leave it empty, so we stepped inside and hit the top button. When it stopped we stepped out and got in another one and went another thirty floors higher until that elevator came to rest. Finally, the only way of getting any higher was to follow a flight or two of stairs, which we did, and found ourselves on the seventy-first floor among planks of wood, scaffolding pipes and heaps of builders' rubble. Everything was covered in dust. The windows were so dusty, I had to open one and stick my head out, desperately clinging on to my trusty old Leica camera. Oh, but the views!

After ten minutes I was lost in the excitement of it all, and completely unaware that an extremely irate foreman had burst on the scene and was threatening Simon with blue murder, in an Irish accent. We pretended to be innocent tourists fresh from Ireland, hoping he would soften and show us around. Not a bit of it! 'I could lose my job over this,' he exploded, going on about just how dangerous it was, thumbing in my direction after my Fay Wray act dangling out of the window. 'No buts, no questions, out, *now!*' Grateful that he hadn't literally thrown us out, as it was over eight hundred feet to the street below, we laughed like naughty schoolboys all the way down in the elevators. Oh well, I did manage to take some photographs.

Finding those old colour transparencies recently in a cardboard box buried deep in a chaotic archive, I

External view of the Chrysler Building

56

now realise what a privileged glimpse we'd been given of an architectural gem, albeit rather dishevelled. Until it closed in 1945, the seventy-first floor had been the public observatory, designed in the art deco style, with sloping walls as the building narrowed towards the spire, and beautiful globe-shaped hanging lights with rings around them based on the planet Saturn. You can see what it was like from a few faded black and white photographs easily found on the internet, but more recently this scene was lovingly reconstructed on a sound stage in Hollywood as a set for the movie *The Aviator*. Alec Baldwin plays Juan Trippe, head of Trans World Airlines, whose office in the Chrysler Building is recreated for the movie.

I find it interesting that of all the hundreds of truly fabulous photographs of the Chrysler Building on the internet, only a handful show the *interior* of the top floors, or views looking *out* from those iconic triangular windows. It's all very exclusive, it seems, even to this day. It was

pretty exclusive back in the 1930s: two floors below the one we trespassed onto belonged to the Cloud Club. Men-only members paid two hundred dollars' membership for the privilege of dining in such exquisite surroundings. Guys like Juan Trippe himself, the publisher Condé Nast and Gene Tunney, the famous boxer whose parents came from Kiltimagh in County Mayo, were regular members. In 1934, Margaret Bourke-White had difficulty getting permission from Walter Chrysler to photograph her famously daring shots sitting on the sixtieth-floor gargoyles because she was a woman.

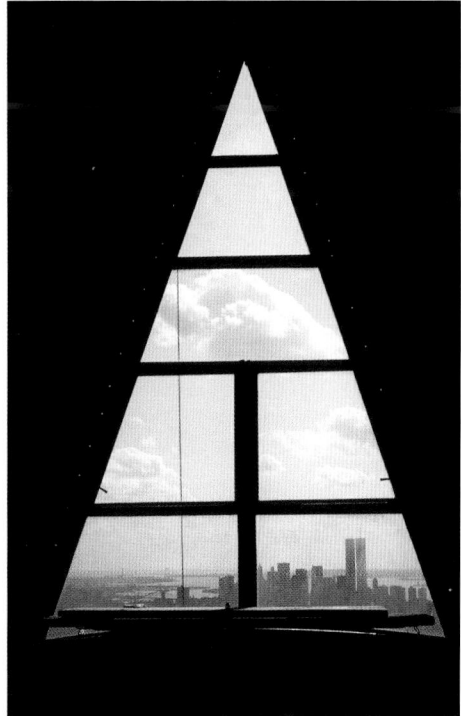

The view from the Chrysler Building toward the World Trade Centre

The 71st floor of the Chrysler Building in the 1930s

The floors above the seventy-first, had we managed to escape the clutches of the foreman, would have revealed the unoccupied, ever-decreasing spaces housing the gigantic water tanks, elevator motors and cabling. Above that floor, you're into the spire itself with its steel ladders and a toilet which, in 1930, must have been the highest loo in the world! It's all very draughty up there, and they had

Looking out from the Chrysler Building

terrible problems with leaks from the rain (I hope it was rain!), according to some architects who had offices in the high-sixties floors. But it didn't seem to bother Dr Weiss, a pioneer of implant technology who had a dental practice up on the sixty-ninth until 2012 and was known as 'the dentist in the sky'.

On the 71st floor of the Chrysler Building with Simon

The photographs show a view south to downtown Manhattan, with the ill-fated Twin Towers clearly visible on the skyline, and in the distance the Verrazzano-Narrows Bridge linking Brooklyn with Staten Island. The view looking out one of the north-facing windows shows another landmark a few blocks away: the City Group Building, with its distinctive forty-five degree roof.

So what makes the Chrysler Building so special and well loved, even among hard-nosed New Yorkers? The building owes much of its fame and glamour to the shiny metal coating with its polished silver look and rows of pointed windows that form a fan pattern at the top. While it glints in the sun by day, at night the pretty art deco design is picked out in lights. The effect is simply stunning. It's a fairly conventional building up to the sixty-first floor, built with over three million bricks. However, from there on skywards you have a completely hand-crafted construction, mainly of steel and sheet metal, all put together in workshops on the sixty-fifth and sixty-sixth floors. It's a bit like wearing a diamond tiara with jeans. Each arc of triangular windows is a slightly different shape to the arc below, and that's why you can tell exactly which windows in my photographs match up to the exterior design.

The seventy-first floor is still closed and unoccupied, apparently, and that's a pity – although it is in better condition than when we found it. Maybe the reason for the closure is no different now to why it closed in the first place. When the Empire State Building opened in 1931, with its open-air viewing deck, almost overnight the Chrysler's observatory and tiny windows became a poor second in terms of viewing Manhattan, and the number of visitors dropped off dramatically.

In the late 1990s I made a photomontage using one of these views as a background and superimposed a photo I'd taken of a car I found in San Francisco plastered with stuck-on toys and dolls. I called it 'Manhattan Toyride'. Right now, in 2025, I'm dreaming of an artist's studio up there with the gods, even if only for a few weeks. I wouldn't mind the draughts and leaks – honestly I wouldn't. How about it, Mr Chrysler? Oh, and Mr Chrysler, I promise not to mention that you refused to pay the architect, William Van Alen, his fee and that he had to sue you for it!

Back to Portugal

Returning from America, where everything worked, our outfit back in Portugal appeared to be dilapidated and hanging by a thread. Pete and Maria Joao had organised a tour of the north of Portugal so that kept us going for another month. We started with a week of shows in Porto which included an invitation to do a ten minute 'clown football game' during half time at Porto football club's first game of the season. The crowd of twenty-five thousand didn't seem to be much interested at first as we all stood around the middle of the field in a motley assortment of costumes until, that is, a giant ball that had been carried on to the pitch and placed in the centre spot started to move without anyone being near it. When the ball split in half and Paddy jumped out of it carrying a real football which he started kicking towards one of the goals the crowd got interested.

Of course, we all tried to stop him from scoring with useless attempts to tackle him so by the time he arrived at the empty goal, he had dribbled round all ten of us and all he had to do was slot it into the net. He sent the ball wide which wasn't supposed to happen but it managed to raise the biggest laugh from the delighted crowd. I don't think the two teams playing the proper game had been told we were going to be doing a show while they were off the field, so when they appeared to resume the game they stood on the sidelines, gawping at the creatures leaving the field. I've boasted many times since that I've played at a first division game on Porto's home ground.

A festival in Vila Nova de Cerveira welcomed the company for an extended stay by the banks of the Minho river. We washed in the river and swam across to Spain if we fancied a Spanish omelette at the cafe on the other side. Enormous yellow flying boats dropped on to the water, scooped up thousands of litres of water in a few seconds and took off again, dropping the water on some distant forest fire where a pall of smoke hung over northern Spain.

In those simple, wholesome days without TV or radio, if I got tired of listening to music or drawing, I would just take one of the dogs and go walking in the mountains. I adored one of the border collies, Ufo, and she'd sometimes seek me out, eager for a nice long walk, especially if her owners, Rod and Charmian, went off shopping in the city. If it wasn't a walk it would be the tireless exercise of fetching something. She would place a nice rounded stone between my feet and refer to it with her head cocked to one side, looking at me then the stone. If the stone didn't get thrown she would rush at it with her front paws and if that didn't work she'd pick it up and gently place it on top of my shoe and whine at it. Of course, if it *was* thrown she had it back at my feet again within seconds and if it landed in a stream or even the ocean, she eventually returned, prancing triumphantly with something similar enough to fool me.

One evening when I took one of our other dogs, Chica, along with a local dog who was looking for some action, we continued walking in the hills all through the night. It was a stretch too far for the dogs, and by daybreak they had started whining and looking at me imploringly. I would encourage them with an enthusiastic voice to chivvy them along and made sure we all drank plenty of water. When we got back to camp they fell in a heap and happily conked out on the baked earth. I went for a swim in the river,

Simon with Elsebeth and Henry

which I needed badly to refresh myself. After only a couple of minutes in the water my exhausted body gave up, as if someone had taken the batteries out and I suddenly lost all power. I was convinced that the river's gathering surge was taking me to the ocean and there was nothing I could do about it. I called out to a guy fishing up ahead on the river bank, spluttering in a panic because my head was going under too many times.

As he seemed to get closer I could make out that he was chuckling. *Hey! I'm drowning here and all he can do is laugh at me* was the only thing going through my head. What's the Portuguese for help? 'Ajuda!' He was still smiling when the river itself deposited me at his feet. Sheepishly, I dragged myself onto the grassy bank and crawled away on my hands and knees before he had the chance to throw me back in.

WHILE OUT SHOPPING AT THE VILLAGE supermarket one morning I bumped into Caroline, so I offered to help with her laden bags while she carried her daughter, Amy. Two years old, blonde-haired and with a sunny nature, Amy was what the Irish call a dote. She didn't have much of a vocabulary. In fact she was quite content to limit herself to a big 'hello', drawing out the 'o' as English people do, followed by a big fat smile. Okay, so she did have the odd bout of crying (didn't we all?) that sounded like a Second World War air raid siren, but on the whole she was great.

It was another lovely late summer morning, before the heat of the day arrived. It was already September and the light was changing, strengthening the shadows that fell from the buildings across the cobbled streets. As we walked in contented silence down the street, Amy fixed her gaze on something from her vantage point looking over Caroline's shoulder. She slowly raised her arm and, reaching out, pointed to our left where an archway framed a long, dark passage. In a strangely serious and sombre tone, Amy said, 'Egyptian in there.'

Caroline and Amy

A shiver went down the back of my neck and the hairs stood on my forearms like a brush. All three of us looked at each other, then back down the passage where Amy was still pointing, and then 'Aaaaar!!' we ran as fast as carrying a child and bags of shopping would allow until we reached the edge of the village at the bottom of the hill. It was only then that Caroline and I checked with each other, 'Did you hear the same thing I heard?' Yes, we both did, but whatever she saw, sensed or imagined, it remained Amy's secret.

While the stay in Cerveira had been a lot of fun, we had a hepatitis scare and everyone had to be tested. It was the only time I could remember the entire company assembling at the ungodly hour of eight o'clock in the morning, as we all did at the local clinic before leaving for Lisbon.

The Story of Phil Oldaker

Phil was one of those unfortunate boys who, after years of neglect and punishment from parents and foster parents, completed the juvenile part of his life in a care home for delinquent children. So when he was given the chance to join the famous Cornish barn-stormers, Footsbarn Travelling Theatre, in 1980 when he was about sixteen, he relished the opportunity to become an apprentice of sorts as an electrician. He had the job of helping the technicians, who gave him the nickname 'Plug'.

Phil carried his painful past in the form of a rigid leg, and although I'd heard that doctors were mystified by it, I never questioned him about it and nobody ever saw that leg bend at the knee. The resulting hobbled walk didn't stop him from doing anything, mind you. He could climb a ladder and even play football with a strange, awkward agility. Even his slightly guilty demeanour and crooked teeth were softened by eyes with the most beautiful long, dark lashes, and that saved him from being an out-and-out 'scruffian'.

Although I was nearly twice his age, he was always cheeky to me, and because he had been with the company over a year when I joined he treated me like a complete novice. What was worse was that he had expert knowledge about the truck that I was going to be driving, even though he was too young to drive it himself. This enormous truck carried the tent, including the king poles and all the paraphernalia that goes with a big white canvas theatre marquee. He told me how the truck was built for carrying telephone poles over the moors in Cornwall, where it had already served one lifetime before the theatre company acquired it.

Warwick, the previous driver, gave me a rudimentary tour of the truck, cab and mechanicals then left me to it. I stood in front of it as a rookie bullfighter might stare down his first bull, full of bravado but quaking inside. Someone with experience had made a painted wooden sign and fixed it to the radiator grille. In jolly circus lettering it said, 'The Brute'.

My first attempt at taming this leviathan was one late September afternoon when the sun was still beating down on the Barcelona streets. We had spent the previous three weeks performing on a baked and dusty site in the heart of the city. On this scorching afternoon we left the city needing only to crawl our way fifteen miles up the coast to Canet de Mar, where our Catalan friends, Els Comediants, were throwing a party. However, the bone-shaking experience of driving The Brute had left me with a headache so bad the only thing I wanted to do was put my head in a bucket of ice. Phil seemed highly amused, and winced with mock pain every time the gears growled. He bellowed instructions from his throne in the passenger seat. He explained that the mountain of blankets between our two seats concealed the metal engine cover, served as insulation from the engine's heat and also reduced the deafening noise in the cab. In winter, he added, the blankets were discarded to gain some heat at the expense of an increase in decibels from the engine, which then turned into an intolerable din. The thought of it increased the pounding inside my head.

Phil's knowledge came to the rescue one day when Joe in the Magirus Deutz truck up ahead led us all up an incredibly steep hill that turned out to be a dead end. When I saw him turning the truck around at the top of the hill, I started sweating. Stationary and only halfway up to the hilltop where we could turn The Brute, I held on to the handbrake for dear life, hoping that this beast could cope with such a severe incline. Phil sensed my panic and shouted at me to use the crawler gear.

Crawler gear? I didn't know The Brute had one. I found it in a slot opposite the reverse gate, took my right foot off the brake pedal and simultaneously let go of the handbrake and let the clutch out. The Brute took a giant leap up the hill like a kangaroo on steroids.

The fifteen tons of contents in the back took a second to catch up, then thunderously crashed down before settling with a strange hissing sound like something had been punctured. Phil was whooping and cheering as if he was riding a bronco at the rodeo. I looked at him in amazement and burst out laughing. I tried again, taking it gently with the clutch. The immense power took the truck slowly up to the top with no hands or feet on the controls, while Phil sat proudly on his shotgun throne, delighted with himself for saving the day. Jamie told me the next day that it was a spare battery that had been punctured, so no great damage done.

As the theatre company roamed across the Iberian peninsula that year, and 1981 turned to 1982, I eventually got used to The Brute and grew fond of my impudent passenger. Respite from both of them came in July, when the company was invited to the World Theatre Festival in Denver, Colorado. Having accepted an invitation to fly out there for five weeks, we were told that only the actors and a skeleton crew could travel. Phil was forced to stay behind at a base camp in northern Portugal along with the children, cooks, school teachers, and several of the musicians and crew, together with all the buses, trucks and caravans. Even the tent stayed behind, but I went as part of the administrative team.

When we returned to Portugal, refreshed and inspired from the visit to midwest America, even the sky seemed small, and our trucks looked dinky and toylike compared to the sixteen-wheelers we had seen out on the American highways. The resourceful party left behind at base camp had set up a thriving cafe by the Minho river, where all the crew, women and children, most of whom were also talented musicians, had joined the locals and generally had a busman's holiday. They called the place the 'Cafe Come Late', a nice play on words as *café com leite* in Portuguese means coffee with milk, and it stayed open well into the night.

Phil had found himself a cat. He had clearly fallen in love with it and wanted to take it with us. It was a scrawny-looking young tabby in need of a few weeks' feeding. Since it looked something like Phil himself, it was no wonder he had taken a shine to it, but I could foresee grief ahead, as it was time to mobilise and move south to Lisbon. Sure enough, no end of reasoning about the absurdity of taking a cat on the road would convince Phil to part with his feline friend. I knew we had three or four dogs in the company at the last count, but a travelling cat? No way!

When the morning came for the wagons to roll and everything was packed away in The Brute, and Phil was busy throwing the last of the bicycles on top of the great white whale of a tent in the back of the truck, we prepared to say goodbye to his cat. I decided we would leave it at the fish market in Viana. I left Phil, the most macho of young gurriers, down on the ground in his scruffy denim jacket, saying farewell in sweet and loving tones, one leg stuck out stiffly at an angle, the other tucked underneath him. As I glanced in the truck's rear-view mirror and started the engine, the cat sat peacefully, if somewhat bemused, on his own, sniffing the fish-scented air.

As we set off on the road to Braga some forty miles away, Phil sat in silence, kept his face turned away from me and let the engine do the talking for a change. I caught a glimpse of those eyelashes working overtime, so I left him alone and concentrated on the driving. For an hour and a half we climbed up and down the hills and country roads of northern Portugal. By the time we arrived in Braga, where we'd stop for lunch, he still hadn't spoken. As the dust settled, a glorious silence replaced the metallic roaring of the engine. If they say that the best thing about buying shoes that are too small is the feeling of relief when you take them off, then in the same way I always looked forward to the sound of silence when The Brute's engine cut out and you could hear yourself think again and relax while the engine slowly cooled, as it did that lunchtime in Braga – until it meowed!

Meowed? 'What the hell was that? Phil, you threw the cat in the back of the truck, didn't you?'

In a flash he was busy round the back of the truck trying to scramble over the circus-style advertising board that acted as a tailgate. But even after the tailgate had been removed and no cat emerged, Phil was still protesting his innocence as the plaintive cry persisted. We then looked underneath the truck, and there, behind the back axle, hanging upside-down from a wooden crossbeam, was Phil's cat, who was clearly annoyed at being forced to travel steerage all the way from Viana. Phil had no idea that the cat had jumped aboard; I could see that from the look on his face.

It took us a good five minutes to release the poor crossbeam from the cat's bear hug. Each embedded claw took some skill to remove, especially as the risk of getting scratched from his freed paws increased as we released them. When the two of them were reunited, I felt glad and maybe a little ashamed because I hadn't realised just how much these two likeable rogues had needed each other.

'You're going to have to give it a name now,' I said as we set off on the rocky road to Lisbon.

And so it came to pass, against all the received wisdom – and maybe even because of his own recent experience – the cat sat nodding peacefully for many hundred miles on his blanket on top of the roaring engine cover, happy in the knowledge that it was really he, Hercules the Cat, who had tamed The Brute.

Lisbon

I really loved Lisbon, the 'white city'. I hung out in the old parts, especially around Lapa, Estrela and Bairro Alto. I thought it was beautiful and seedy at the same time. I photographed the eighty-year-old trams that trundled up and down the cobbled streets, and the characters who rode them. I loved the plaintive sound of the knife sharpener's whistle as he went around pushing his bike, the pedals of which spun the grinding stone. I took a liking to the habit of drinking tiny cups of Brazilian coffee, *bica*, at almost any time of

Ted in Lisbon trying to drum up publicity with one of the many hand-made, silk screen posters – Never mind the bulbous cheeks, check out the lump in my neck that caused the health scare that summer (Photo: Pete Smith)

the day. I had a friend, Carmo, who was like a second mother to me and got me in to see the medical specialists ahead of the waiting list. In short, if God had spoken from the heavens and told me I had to live there for the rest of my days, I wouldn't have been disappointed.

One morning I sat next to a friend in her apartment waiting for her to finish a late breakfast, eager to get things moving. I needed her help with publicity, as my Portuguese was very limited. A girlfriend of hers popped in and joined us at the table just when I thought we were ready to go. This one got out all her accoutrements for taking a dose of heroin and started the little ritual, asking me if I wanted to join her. I looked at her and caught a glimpse of the pretty girl she probably once was, but then the dark circles under her eyes made me realise she was going down fast. A terrible sadness filled me to the point that I made an instantaneous vow to myself that I would never take heroin, and thankfully I never have. We left her to it and seized the day.

The Swiss movie *Dans la Ville Blanche* (*In the White City*) was showing at one of the city cinemas, so Simon and I went to see it. Set almost entirely in Lisbon, it starred Bruno Ganz as a sailor walking around the city; a lot of it was shot on a Super 8 cine camera, which was just perfect for Lisbon, and it seemed to capture the essence of the old city. Unfortunately for Simon, it also starred a Portuguese actor whose ex-girlfriend Simon was now living with, and it reminded him of the painful experience some months earlier when, in a fit of jealousy, this guy had stabbed Simon through the hand. Understandably, it was too much for Simon to watch, and he walked out.

On a more positive note, the specialist I saw in Lisbon put my mind at rest after the test results on the lump in my neck had come back. It proved to be a benign cyst, and the advice was to leave it alone. It's still there, shrunk to about half the size over time. I wasn't overly surprised by this diagnosis, because I had been born with a lymphangioma or cystic hygroma, a huge abnormal mass on the left side of my neck, which was surgically removed when I was eighteen months old. There is only one photograph of me as a baby, taken from the other side. Actually, there are now two because when I was about 45 my aunt gave me a photo she'd taken of me on the beach in 1952 on Anglesey and I saw for the first time what the hygroma had really looked like. I could see why my parents weren't keen to have pictures taken, but the comforting thing was that the holiday snap clearly showed that this little chappie was as happy as a sand boy, as they say.

Spain Again

Bidding a fond farewell to Lisbon for the last time in October 1982 was a little sad, but we had been stuck in Portugal for nearly a year. We finally got a chance to work at another festival, with an invitation to Zaragoza in northern Spain. Once again we would bump into our friends Els Comediants, only this time we would see them performing in their own backyard with the show that became a cult classic, *The Devils*.

On the night we arrived, I was having a drink at a crowded bar with Joe and Phil when I got distracted by a gorgeous Spanish girl who started talking to me. We were enjoying a nice long conversation when, out of the blue, she put her hand on my arm and said, 'Do you want fuckee fuckee?' Oh no! Here we go, I'm back in Spain and I can't even recognise the sex workers! She *was* beautiful, and who was I to judge, but I was so disappointed.

The first time I saw Els Comediants back in Freiburg the previous year I was impressed, but when I encountered them in Zaragoza, it all made so much more sense. In Germany they were enthusiastically received by an appreciative audience who clapped and cheered, but here in Spain the reaction was on another level. Comediants had created little devils and creatures on skates, spitting fire and setting off bangers, rip raps and Roman candles if not exactly in your face then certainly in your direction. The audience members rushed them, just as they do at the bull run in Pamplona. Here, the excitement was ramped up because the event was interactive, which turned it into shrieking exhilaration in the form of a dangerous game. The smell of burning hair and clothes filled the night air. I vowed that someday I would get this company to go to Galway.

These happy autumn days and nights came to an end when we moved down to Valencia. We were greeted on the way by a deluge of torrential rain that went on for days, causing a major dam burst that made thousands of people homeless in the region. It was also the week that the country's general election was gearing up for a final campaign blitz. I despaired because my hand-printed posters were lovingly posted around the city in the morning only to be obliterated in the afternoon by an army of rival campaigners vying for every inch of public space. No one was interested in a rapidly dilapidating travelling theatre.

A week later it was November and, hoping to revive the success of our previous visit to Granada twelve months before, we set up in the grounds of the university once again. But who should arrive in town at the same time? None other than Pope John Paul II himself, and competing with his publicity was hopeless. Not to be outdone, I still went round the city putting up posters, especially around the places and bars where the students hung out.

I was just tearing down an out of date circus poster that was proving to be stubborn when two young guys reeled out of a bar door a few feet away. One was clearly the worse for drink and staggered to the edge of the pavement where he threw up the contents of his stomach into the night air, landing it neatly in the gutter with a resounding splat. The other one had wandered off still chatting away to him, but then realised his mate wasn't there by his side. Turning back just in time to see the last of the diced carrots flying through the air, he came to his friend's rescue saying, 'O bueno' in comforting tones and rested his hand on the poor fella's back.

I returned my attention to the ripped circus poster where I'd managed to remove the name and dates but the circular image in the centre where a horse's head remained, tenaciously adhered to the wooden door. I'd created an illusion with the torn shreds of the poster which made it look as if the horse was going even faster. I glued one of our posters in another place, leaving the horse to live another day, and went on my weary way.

The tent flooded twice in three weeks, and the first snow fell on the Sierra Nevada mountains beyond the Alhambra palace. It was effing freezing and we had to use a space heater in the tent. Weird things kept happening, one after another.

Circus poster remnant in Granada

There was a dull brass instrument that used to get passed around during music sessions. Gregg said it was an 'A flat' horn, and he managed to get the best sound out of it. One day Steve piped up, saying we could all rest assured about the name of the A-flat horn now because Simon had just reversed his truck over it. It was going to be *a flat horn* for the rest of its days, and *nobody* would get a sound out of it.

Then a local Spanish child claimed she'd been bitten by one of our dogs and came down with the police pointing at Ufo. Rabies was fairly common in Spain, so the police said they were going to take our dogs away. All hell broke loose as men, women and children, mostly our lot, screamed and shouted so vehemently that it looked at one stage as though the police might get nervous enough to resort to arms. Ten-year-old Bibo desperately clung on to Ufo around the neck and would have been dragged all the way to the station, so determined was she to save the dog from being put down. I'd never seen poor Ufo look so petrified as she searched everyone's faces in turn as if to say, 'I didn't do anything! I don't know this girl, you've got to believe me!' Somehow it got resolved and, with warnings from the police, everything calmed down and the dogs got a reprieve.

The tent looked anything but inviting. From the outside we must have looked a sorry sight, and so, to their enormous credit, the Andalusian gypsies bailed us out with a generous gift of cash. A lot of cash. The starlit party we had with them round the campfire was all music and dancing and (of course) raw flamenco. If I hadn't been there myself to experience it, I would probably have scoffed at its romantic appeal. But in truth, it was like a scene that Goya could have painted. The girl who got up and sang like Carmen herself left an image to fall in love with. Later, I asked one of the gypsy guys what her name was. He was looking into the fading embers of the fire, telling me to move this log here, and then that one. The fire was now going nicely. I offered him my stick so he could do it. 'No,' he said, 'it doesn't do to poke another man's fire.' And then he winked at me and said, 'Her name is Maria del Mar.'

I might have gone to sleep that night whispering her name into the pillow, but I knew very well that the magic that performers create can be fleeting or elusive. Show people create images that flicker in the limelight, making tantalising moments with live performance. But it's not a good idea to look too closely behind the curtain or the mask. We had our own acting beauties, like Maggie, Margaret and Pureza. Their skills and charms had filled many a man's dreams. Maybe it's something to do with the essence of theatre itself, going back to ancient times, and the nature of capture and rapture in an unspoken contract between the performer and the audience. We have an ingrained willingness to suspend belief and ridicule, because we *want* to be caught hook, line and sinker. In my case it was a pretty girl with a beautiful voice in a magical setting. The more powerful the performance, the easier it is to be lost in the rapture. I was happy enough to cherish a memory rather than go chasing the girl. Now, forty years later, I can still recall the Goya painting I captured with my mind's eye. And yes, the painting moves and sings.

A DAY OFF! YAY! LET'S GO TO PRADOLLANO. A bunch of us took a trip above the snow line high into the Sierra Nevada mountains. We piled into our school bus and piled out again a couple of hours later at the tourist stop in sparkling fresh snow. I did say 'trip', and I did mean 'high'. It was one of only two occasions in my life when I took LSD. I took the tabs on the bus, and by the time we got to the tourist cafe they were beginning to take effect. I was having trouble looking at some workmen further down the line waiting for coffee. It was their brand-new blue overalls, their *bleu de travail*, that made my eyes dazzle. I know it sounds silly, but I had to get out of there, so I set off alone in the sun and snow with only my black tee shirt, jeans and runners.

I must have climbed for an hour through the snow with boundless energy. I was thirty-two and pretty fit. I followed the Sol y Neve ski trail higher and higher fixing my stare on the prize of Veleta's summit. In the warm sunshine it turned into a mirage, so now it was a giant baked Alaska in a blue heaven. Eventually, I reached a ridge where I stopped to survey the scene and look back down at the people scurrying like ants way below. About fifty metres away from me on the same ridge, two engineers were fixing an isolated antenna, so I ploughed over to them and asked in Spanish how long it would take to get up there, pointing at Veleta's craggy peak. The conversation was very short. They had an imploring look in their eyes that went on and on as time seemed to come to a halt, and still I gazed longingly at the meringue pie in the sky, then back at the two faces. It was the emphasis they put on the word *morir* that I wasn't too happy with. They weren't going to stop me! Or maybe they were. I decided that discretion was the better part of valour and went back down, mulling over what they had said in my befuddled head.

'*Si subes allí, vas a morir.*'

'If you go up there, you're going to die.'

Yes, I could have reached the summit in about four hours, but by then night would have been closing in and temperatures falling fast below zero. In tee shirt and jeans? It was like my first day in Portugal revisited. I had a great day but, who knows, I might owe my life to those two engineers, and I never took acid again.

Skin-deep in Jerez

The whole town sits silently, soaked in sherry. The intoxicating smell gets into your nostrils and stays there no matter where you walk. The town in southwest Spain that gave its name to the region's famous and distinctive fortified wine is Jerez de la Frontera. The British called it 'sherry'. Strangely, by the end of that autumn in 1982, touring the region's towns and villages, my own skin turned a deep tan, similar to the colour of Amontillado sherry.

Many of the old narrow streets of Jerez are cobbled and lined with whitewashed houses. The grander houses have walled front gardens, and some have elegant courtyards and exquisite tiles with Moorish designs in blue, yellow and white. Ornate wrought-iron gates keep you at arm's length from orange trees laden with fruit and scent. I was amazed to find that they fruit and flower at the same time, but the sweet scent of orange blossom struggled with the all-pervading smell of sherry.

As an artist and painter, I was so inspired by the colour palette of this classic Andalusian paintbox. I loved the contrast of colours against the white walls, the shiny dark-green leaves of the orange trees, the black ironwork, the blue ceramics and the terracotta roof tiles. Add to this the sultry silence of a pleasantly warm November Sunday afternoon, perfect for a solo stroll around town, with the summer's punishing heat long forgotten, I was in a state of perambulating bliss. The only sound was from a caged canary singing somewhere, out of sight around the corner. Turning that corner, I was in a mini-world of whiteness, walking under endless rows of pure-white bed sheets softly hanging out to dry, without a breath of wind to stir them high above the street, blotting out the deep blue sky.

The shadow of a young woman passed inside a window, and I noticed a pair of eyes briefly alight on me while the rest of the house slept on through siesta. I was reminded of the line from a song that James

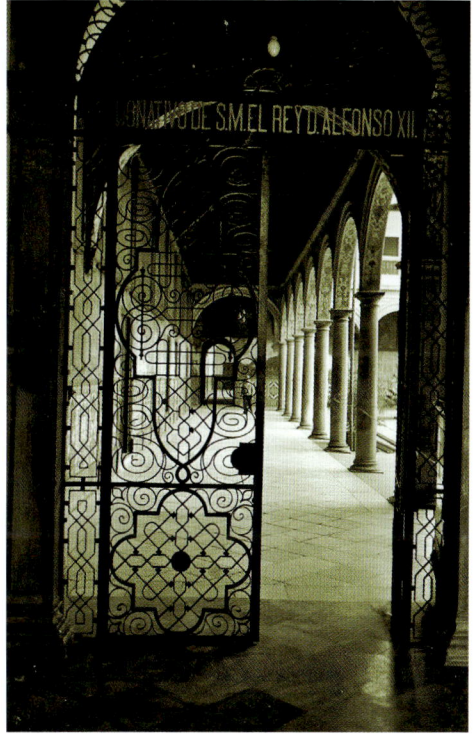

Beautiful wrought iron work, typical in Spain at the time

Joyce quotes near the end of *Ulysses* as Molly Bloom reflects on her time in Gibraltar: 'Glancing eyes a lattice hid for her lover to kiss the iron'. I was confused by it when I read it, but now I think I understand it for the first time. Well, here's one possible explanation.

Here in Jerez, a dark-eyed Spanish beauty clearing the lunch table glances outside where, I imagine, she sees her lover loitering with intent in the shadow of the sunlight, lest he be seen. 'Pssst!' he calls, trying to get her attention. She dares not look again in case her rampant heart, beating in her chest and ears, gets so loud that her mother will hear it. Her mother need not worry: the lovers are separated by a wrought-iron grille that defends the window, typical in Spain, so that the young man, desperate to express his passion, can only kiss the cold iron lattice as her warm lips are, for now, out of reach.

Suddenly the apparition dissolved and I found myself walking on alone. But not quite alone, it seemed. Turning another corner, I came across a similar young couple. While the houses dozed in the dumb indolence of the siesta hours, the lovers took advantage with a secret rendezvous. Even from the far end of the street, I could tell they were besotted with each other. They were completely lost in each other's gaze, and as she pressed her body against his, pinning him against the cool white wall, she cradled his face with her hands. They hardly noticed me as I approached, trying to mind my own business. It wasn't until I was almost level with them that I noticed what her intimate attentions were really about. She was squeezing blackheads out of his face!

Trying to shake the image out of my head, I hurried on and turned another corner, where I was able to let out a snort of laughter. But then I noticed a woman calling enthusiastically from the open door in a row of simple white houses right on the street. Who, me? There was no one else in sight. '*Ven aqui, ven aqui,*' she said, beckoning with her fingers pointing downward. (Making the same gesture with the fingers pointing upward is thought to be rude in southern Europe.)

Her bright red dress and matching lip gloss should have been a warning, but it wasn't until I peered in through the front door and realised what I had stumbled into. Shielding my brow from the sunlight, I stared into the gloom where the tiny den was crammed with over-stuffed sofas and over-sized women. They all beamed at me and seemed so eager to introduce themselves that it looked like a competition. Again, the contrast of colours screamed from the gaudy dresses, the jet-black hair, the gleaming white shiny teeth and over-done make-up. I was suddenly terrified. I was going to be eaten by black widow spider-women after performing some torrid final act. I politely made my excuses and, after clumsily backing out, scurried away, choosing a parting of ways over parting with money, no matter how many parting legs were on offer.

AFTER THE COMPANY HAD DONE A WEEK'S performances of full-house shows at the behest of the Jerez local council, who generously covered the entire run so that we could throw the doors open to the public for free, we also did a number of small events for the villagers all around the region. They had been working all the daylight hours and even beyond, into the night, with the grape harvest for that year. The entertainment was a welcome break for what seemed like arduous work.

It also gave us the opportunity to experience true flamenco one afternoon in Sanlúcar de Barrameda, when a masterclass of unadulterated flamenco music was delivered in spadefuls by an amazing Spanish guitarist accompanied by his own passionate voice. The whole cultural shebang was an astounding lesson. The way that this rural Andalusian audience, nearly all wearing their Sunday black best, had been transfixed by every song was a sight and sound to remember. It made me realise where the likes of Rodrigo's Concerto de Aranjuez had come from, and that to hear it played on any instrument other than guitar made no sense whatsoever. I was told that most male flamenco musicians sing songs about their lovers, their mothers or death. I could see how Hemingway had become so attracted to the culture and its macho baselines. I never went to a bullfight like the ones that Hemingway seemed to enjoy, but I did once raise a glass to an old poster, lovingly preserved in a bar in Linares, the place where Spain's legendary matador Manolete performed his last act before the Miura bull Islero gored him to death.

As the old year came to an end, the results of the elections came through. The Jerez socialist council had been ousted, and the new council refused to pay us.

After we left Jerez I never drove The Brute again. Somehow it found its way back to Baranco in Portugal, where I found it a year later on a holiday visit. I felt bad that I'd never said goodbye, as if it was a friend of Thomas the Tank Engine's or something. There it was, hidden in the eucalyptus forest at the end of a sandy track, its life rounded with a little sleep before it decayed into the ground.

I found a couple of my old posters in the back advertising a gig in Lisbon. It gave me the shivers, and I thanked God I didn't have to drive it again.

The Great Escape – An Epic Journey Across Spain

After a long, dispirited meeting in Jerez that first week in December 1982, we all agreed that the company should take a break and regroup in the spring. Some of us stayed in the south of Spain and got by with gigs in local villages and busking. Some of the cooks, mechanics and musicians, and their children, never returned to Footsbarn but went their own ways. Some of us decided to go back to England or, in my case, back to Galway. But getting there at all with very little money was going to be touch and go. It involved an epic journey across the length of the Iberian peninsula from Jerez to Madrid and then north again to Santander where, if we made it, the ferry would take us to Plymouth.

The roads in Spain were not great in those days before the motorways were built, and it was a big ask for Paddy's old Leyland truck. When we set off, it must have looked comical with the caravan teetering along behind, but we didn't care. Paddy, Freddy, Josie and Petal slept in the truck whenever we stopped for the night, while Denis and I slept in the caravan. We were absurdly suntanned, that strange amber colour that people turn in southwest Spain.

The journey out of Andalusia was a long and arduous grind, winding across hills and great sweeping valleys where rows of ancient olive trees hugged the folds and waves of the rolling landscape in regimented lines, like lollypops stuck in a patchwork quilt. When we reached Toledo the sky was dappled with fluffs of high white cloud, the kind you only see on a large land mass like Iberia. I tried to imagine being El Greco, the painter who spent a lot of his working life here, and so it was not such a strange coincidence that we found his paintings in a local church where he'd painted his trademark elongated figures below the exact same sky we'd just seen.

On and on we crawled, stopping in Valdepeñas to fill up the empty *garrafóns* with ridiculously cheap wine, and on through La Mancha where we saluted the roadside statues of Don Quixote and Sancho Panza, acknowledging that our quest, too, was in tatters.

Josie needed to get her passport sorted out at the British Embassy in Madrid, so after Toledo we continued north all the while rising in altitude, on and on until the metropolis came in to view and then into the heart of the capital city. The embassy, like many other diplomatic buildings, was in a pleasant and leafy part of old Madrid. We found a space big enough to park the truck and its caravan right in front. The truck looked rather jaunty with its pretty, circus-style sign writing emblazoned down the side. Or at least we thought so, even if it was a little out of place in such a neighbourhood. Strangely, an embassy official thought it was out of place too. Before Paddy could get Josie ready to go inside, the man was already into the old 'You can't park that thing here' routine.

When you have spent a year and a half in the company of decent, gentle country folk speaking Spanish and Portuguese, the sudden sound of a pompous British civil servant's voice can be a little irksome. Paddy ignored him, and the rest of us grinned through the window of the truck. The man went off inside but returned almost immediately with a uniformed soldier who carried a machine gun. I said, 'I think you'd better move the truck, Paddy.' Well, there just happened to be a space on the opposite side of the street, where a man stood guard in front of another consulate building. We asked in Spanish if we could park there. 'Sí, señor,' he said. After we had spent a few minutes manoeuvring the truck and caravan across the road, the British official turned back inside, ushering the soldier along with him, a sour face on him and steam escaping from his ears. I looked at the plaque on the wall where we had parked. It was the

Argentinian Embassy! Paddy and Josie took themselves off inside the building, where I imagined Paddy would give some other official a good ear-bashing and tell them what to do, as only an actor can.

Would this old Leyland truck get us the rest of the way over the mountains and down to the north coast to make the Santander ferry? Another day's drive lay ahead before we could even contemplate the long ferry crossing to Plymouth. And while we chatted and played games along the way, one ear was on constant alert for any telltale change in the engine's perpetual drone.

Financially broke and with no film left in the camera, we watched beautiful landscapes pass by the window as we climbed through the hills beyond Burgos. As we entered the Cantábrica mountain range, I ached to be able to stop and take photographs. It was time to get out the jumpers and coats, now that the warmth of Andalusia had been left behind. Gone too were the Moorish influences, as more Gothic architecture featured in the towns and villages we passed. Reversing the route that Laurie Lee took in *As I Walked Out One Summer Morning*, we finally caught sight of the sea and coasted down the steep

A photograph of the Footsbarn kids that was subsequently damaged somehow typifies the level of squalor that prevailed at the end of 1982 – Rowan, Rebecca A, Sarah, Alice, Petal and Robert, a visiting friend

country road out of the mountains and into Santander. Freddy cobbled together one last meal of sausages and rice. It was all that was left to feed us.

At last we were on the ferry boat to Blighty, and as the ship slipped away from the harbour into the Bay of Biscay, I settled into the bar and talked to Paddy. The next thing I knew I was throwing up rice and sausages in the loo. Farewell to Spain. It seemed like a fitting end to 1982.

I parted company with Paddy and Freddy and the others when we arrived in Plymouth after hours and hours of rolling, pitching and heaving across the winter sea. They made their way in the truck through the snow to Batworthy farm in Devon. Freddy told me that the truck eventually conked out at the farm cattle grid and flatly refused to make it up the hill to the house. I got a train at Plymouth where people on the platform stared at me. Okay, so I looked like a gypsy, with a deep tan and weird clothes for England in December, but I didn't care. I was exhausted and happy to fall into my parents' home for Christmas. An hour in a hot bath works wonders, but it would be a while before the ingrained dirt of months on the roads and dusty sites disappeared and the skin on my face and hands paled from deep amber so that people no longer stared at me.

At new year I went to see my old friends Martin and Susie Parr, who were now living in Wallasey across the Mersey from Liverpool. Martin had completed a series of photographic projects in Ireland, where they had lived for a while, including subjects like abandoned Morris Minors, bad weather and several tourist and pilgrimage sites. He was about to embark on what turned out to be a searing and controversial series, with his own 'middle-class England' in the spotlight. Brilliant!

Looking through Martin's photos of nearby New Brighton, in which people incongruously sunbathed next to giant mechanical diggers, I told him I'd nearly drowned there when I was four, on a day trip with my Mum and Dad and his old army friends. I'd puked all the way home and we never saw Dad's mates again. Martin took a photograph of me at the offending spot where I'd fallen into the boating pool back in 1954.

My parents gave me some money, bless them, and in the new year I went straight back to Galway. Ollie was generous and hospitable as usual. I holed up in his house and got involved with the catering when he put on huge dinner parties. I designed another Galway Arts Festival poster in early March, my fifth poster for the festival, now in its sixth year. Then, suddenly, I went completely deaf in my left ear. The doc said I would have to undergo an operation because a bony lump was growing across the ear canal, causing an infection. A surgeon at University Hospital Galway burred it off with a drill. I wish he hadn't told me that! I only found out by accident when he invited some students to look inside my ear. They took turns to ogle down a scope while he explained to them what he'd done. Anyone who has had an ear operation will tell you that it's one of the most painful things imaginable. Every change of dressing is excruciating, and the thought of a Black & Decker drill going in there to fix it was more than my brain could accept. After the fourth student jostled for the right angle to see anything, the surgeon asked me not to swear so much.

During a boring eight-day stay in hospital, my spirits were lifted by two nurses from Cork who came in laughing one day. I asked them what was so funny. One looked at the other and said, 'Well, we're not supposed to tell, but she just reminded me of something you said when we brought you out of theatre into the recovery room.'

'So what did I say?'

'You were delirious, really, but anyway you said, "Friends, Romans, countrymen, lend me your ears", which we thought was pretty funny, like.'

All that remained was to get myself to Turin in Italy, where Footies were going to reinvent themselves with a slimmed-down company. Flights were expensive in those days, so I had to scam a ride somehow. I happened to bump into the artist Seamus Coleman in Dublin one afternoon and, knowing he had a studio in Milan, I asked on a whim if he had a spare airline ticket to Italy.

Amazingly, he said yes! He had a return portion Dublin to Milan that he wasn't using. I thanked him profusely and went home to forge the ticket with my own name in place of his. It wasn't difficult, believe me. I could hardly contain myself. I had wanted to work in Italy for over ten years, and now I was going to get my chance.

I arrived in Turin late at night getting off a rickety slow train from Milan and found the address of the house at 2.30 in the morning. The wedged Footsbarn trucks in the driveway at the side of the house told me I'd got the right place and the front door was open, but the house was asleep. I found an empty bedroom upstairs and fell into a deep exhausted sleep.

It was the kids who discovered me still asleep in the morning and jumped on me with delight. When they rushed off down the stairs shouting, 'Ted's here, Ted's here', someone replied, 'Well, let him in.'

'No, he's asleep upstairs.'

None of the adults believed them, having fallen for several April Fool's jokes already, until I wandered into the kitchen looking for anything resembling breakfast.

1983: The Year I Always Wanted

John Kilby's call-out to reform Footsbarn in Italy in April 1983 brought together most of the actors and two technicians plus Simon the percussionist, the musician Paul, Charmian the costumier, mask maker Freddy and me – not forgetting several children. We had promises of gigs in Asti in northern Italy and Avignon again in France.

We needed so much new stuff to get back on the road. The old tent, which was so shoddy it had lost any resemblance to its ivory-white canvas beginnings, eventually arose like the firebird, reborn in the form of a shredded, grey cloth backdrop for *King Lear*. Forming a complete theatre set stretched across a steel framework which included cave-like entrances, with the shreds of canvas dangling like stalactites, it could work in both an open-air setting and in conventional theatres. But where was all this work and rehearsal going to be done? We had the loan of a big old house in Turin but it wasn't going to be adequate for all the workshop space we needed.

Turin seemed to me to be an odd introduction to Italy and not exactly the type of place I imagined we'd be working in. I was impressed with the things that it was famous for, sure enough. One couldn't go far in the city without coming across reminders of just how well Juventus was doing in those days, having won the Serie A football league two years in a row the previous seasons, with Liam Brady in the number ten shirt and Trapattoni at the helm. And then, of course Fiat was ever present with its famous car manufacturing plant at Lingotto. Yes, the one with the race track on the roof. But I was slightly dismayed to be told in no uncertain terms at the local restaurant that if I wanted *pizza*, I would need to go to Naples to find it! Sorry I asked. I didn't realise that cuisine was so fiercely regional in Italy.

While the actors read the parts for Shakespeare's *King Lear* holed up in Joe's room in the attic, I came down with a dreadful cold. Fed up with just a sleeping bag on a freezing tiled floor in a room with no furniture, I was in need of something more inspiring. 'It's miserable and damp here. Can we go somewhere else please?' I pleaded to the heavens.

Then, out of the blue, at an outdoor clown show in one of Turin's city piazzas, where our actors did their usual magic, an angel just happened to see the show. This welcoming angel, Maurizia Settembri, was a producer from Pisa who reckoned she could get us

all the work space we needed in a hill town in Tuscany belonging
to a government-funded theatre research centre based in Pontedera.
While the actors ruminated dubiously on another big move south, I
had a good feeling about this offer and knew that John shared that
feeling. Besides, it was Tuscany! What's not to like?

The two of us went down to Volterra, the hill town between
Pisa and Siena, to check it out. On a beautiful May morning, my
thirty-third birthday, we arrived in this medieval vision of sereni-
ty overlooking the green fields of Tuscany and basked in the warm
beauty of it all. It was one of those moments in life that make you
believe that all your days up to this point had been viewed through
some kind of veil. That God, playing one of his little jokes, had
whipped away the shroud and said, 'Ta-daaaa!' – and there, before
your very eyes, was the Garden of Eden in all its splendour. All we
had to do now was convince ourselves that the buildings on offer,
which were part of a still functioning psychiatric hospital, were just
perfect. I'd brought my camera, which was fortunate, because we
had a task on our hands explaining this to the rest of the company.

The rehearsal space set aside for the actors was in another building in the village, away from the hospital. We had a look in. I secretly bagged a space in the foyer for my desk and easel. Right next door
was a cafe. As I stood at the front door, I noticed a man approaching
down the narrow street on a motorbike. As the noise from the bike
got louder I realised he was heading straight for me. When he got
as far as the steps to the cafe, he turned the bike ninety degrees and,
without stopping, mounted the steps and disappeared through the
open door. We were introduced later. He taught me how to catch
flies with my bare hands. It turned out he was the owner of the cafe,
and I remember thinking, I'm going to like this mad place!

From that moment on, I felt at home in Italy. If 1982 had been a
year of many professional frustrations, then 1983 became a year of
fulfilment and fruition and one of the favourite years of my working
life. Pontedera, an unassuming working town known mostly for its

Piaggio scooter factory, was a delight to visit. Having spent so much time in various printing establishments around Europe watching printers make a mess of my work, I was astounded when I discovered Bandecchi & Vivaldi, just around the corner from the research centre in Pontedera, who actually enhanced my paintings with their printed reproductions.

The man himself at the factory, Sergio Vivaldi, seemed to take a shine to me, calling me Teduccio loudly across the clatter of the shop floor whenever I went in with new artwork. This caused all the young women who were packing boxes or shifting pallets to stop, look up and beam at me. My heart would melt because they were all so beautiful and probably sang like Maria Callas, and looking up I couldn't quite avert my eyes from the almost life-size posters of naked Italian glamour models that filled the walls. It was just one of many occasions during my tour of Italy where images of the naked female form were so blatantly exhibited. Leaving the printers, I would drive back to the hill-top retreat in Volterra and fall asleep in my room dreaming that the printer girls were dancing naked in the shadows at the end of the bed.

ONE DAY I TOOK ONE OF THE TRUCKS AND went with Charmian, our costumier, to the town of Empoli by the Arno River, locally famous for its leather industry, to see if they had any scraps or reject pelts that we could have for costumes. We explained that we were doing a theatre show, so they led us to a courtyard where women were grading and sorting pelts and furs.

'Ask the women here. They'll tell you what you can have.' The women pointed to a pile of dozens of rejected leather hides of all kinds and colours. Furs were in a separate pile. When we examined them, there didn't seem to be much wrong, and many were full-size hides. We chose a few and went back to the women to ask if it was okay to take them. They looked a little surprised and confused. They went over to the pile and heaped more furs and sheepskins onto our already laden arms so that we could hardly see where we were going. When we got back to camp and opened up the back of the truck, it looked like we had robbed the factory.

The leather and furs were used by Freddy to make masks and by Charmian to make costumes. They had to be incredibly strong, because so many Footsbarn shows involved multi-characters with a limited number of actors. The actors went through several fast and furious costume changes, so making anything delicate or flimsy was pointless.

Siena and Volterra

Siena was only half an hour away across a ridge of hills. It was top of my list of places to visit – ahead of Florence, even. Volterra was gorgeous, but it was humble compared to Siena. I went there with Carmo, Marta's mother, who had come all the way from Lisbon when Marta was about to bring Giovanni into the world. Carmo had been a godmother to us in Portugal and to me in particular. She saw to it that I had the best medical attention when I got really ill and had to have tests done and see specialists in Lisbon.

As you wander down the narrow streets that circle the centre of Siena, trying to find an entry that leads to the piazza they call the 'Campo' – you know it's there somewhere – and you've seen the photographs but nothing can prepare you for the moment you burst into the bright open space from the dimly shaded streets. You don't get the full reveal until you have found your way out of the maze and down one of the narrow portals that lead to the piazza itself. Once there, the audacious, pencil-thin tower is the first thing that hits you, but it's not until you start looking around that you realise there's not a lot of symmetry here.

The ground slopes from one end to the other in odd geometrical shapes. The piazza itself is neither square, circular nor oblong:

The pencil-thin campanile rising above Siena

it's just odd, and some of the buildings surrounding it are slightly squashed, like a cardboard box pushed out of kilter. And yet everything looks right and in its proper place so that the result is utterly attractive. It may not be as weird as the Leaning Tower in Pisa, but it's just as eccentric and charming. Carmo and I both decided it was one of our favourite places in the world.

After coffee in the May sunshine, we went off to the Duomo, the cathedral built from layers of black and white marble like a liquorice allsort, where the paintings set me off with another fit of gawping and wonderment. I was busy taking photographs in the crowded streets when I became aware of being jostled by an ever-increasing throng of people. Suddenly a horse's head loomed into the camera lens and bellowed 'Forza!' in my face. Lowering the camera, I discovered the horse's handler glaring at me. 'Forza!' he shouted, even louder. Their two heads were side by side; only the horse's was nodding vigorously as if to say, 'Yes, you!' I took this to mean 'Get out of the way, you stupid eejit!' and I stumbled back into the arms of the crowd. It turned out that the Palio horse race was imminent, and one of the competing horses was being paraded around town. After that we were treated to displays of flag-throwing from members of the competing quarters of the municipality. I took this idea into the *King Lear* play by designing huge flags for each of Lear's daughters and one for himself, so the entrance of any one of them was heralded with flag bearers flourishing their own colours and patterns.

Volterra was in a picture postcard setting, with switchback roads lined with spindly cypress trees that led the way up to the terracotta hill town perched high above the Tuscan landscape. When we arrived there in May, the spectacular views revealed a rolling landscape with fields of green grass and purple vetch. By the time we left, six weeks later, the fields were already turning brown, evoking the colours of the paintbox: umber, burnt sienna and yellow ochre.

Julie in Volterra with the waitress from the cafe

The hospital had been a major feature of this small Etruscan town, which was also famous for its alabaster objet d'art. A revolution in mental health care in Italy in the early 1970s had resulted in many patients returning home where possible so that only the more dangerous patients, or those unable to get any home care, remained at the hospital.

We saw many of the patients on a daily basis, either within the grounds or out and about in the village, as several were let out under a strict curfew regime. Okay, so it was a bit scary at times. The very first day, I was awakened at 5.30 in the morning by what sounded like the Muslim call to prayers, before I realised it was someone howling in the hospital building next to us. He did this every morning at the same time, so I got used to it.

One man I saw every day made strange hand signals with his arm resting on top of his head, so he could give you a beady-eyed stare through the upturned V-shape that his fingers made in front of his face. A cocked-wrist, side-to-side motion completed a semaphore-like signal. Of all the hand gestures I ever saw Italians make, this was the most bizarre. He appeared to be a contented soul, with a delightful smile and a cheery wave, often followed by his special signal before he went on his way. That is, until the evening time, when he was always inconsolably sad. I asked about him at the local cafe next to my studio. They said he went to the bus stop every day at four o'clock to meet his mother off the bus, and every day she wasn't there.

Another older man I saw regularly, a bent figure with hands clasped behind his back, kept up a constant banter, punctuated only by a pause to throw his hat on the ground. A momentary state of peace would prevail before he picked up the hat, returned it to his head and resumed the audible chunter.

I found him one afternoon gazing at a large crucifix by the side of the road. It was his interest in it that prompted me to pay attention to something I'd previously walked right past. The crucifix was slightly smaller than life size but still pretty big. The cross itself was made from pieces of steel railway track, while Christ's figure was also constructed from welded metal. The whole thing had rusted from time in the rain. Displayed along the top of the horizontal beam, in minute detail, were all the accoutrements of the carpenter's trade: little mallets and hammers, saws and nails, block planes, rasps and files. It was like the sculptor's little joke.

But what this skilled metalworker made me realise was that back in Jerusalem nearly two thousand years ago a carpenter, ironically, must have made the cross that hanged another fellow carpenter's boy. I turned around and gazed across the most beautiful view I'd ever seen, something that Jesus Christ here, with his eyes cast down in perpetual pain, wasn't able to do. As the old man disappeared down the hill, I could still hear him muttering away in Italian. I looked up at Christ and said I was sorry for his troubles and gave thanks for being alive and, hopefully, sound of mind.

As the actors worked on the rehearsals for the play, naturally the characters began to take shape, and

Sketch of Dave J as Lear

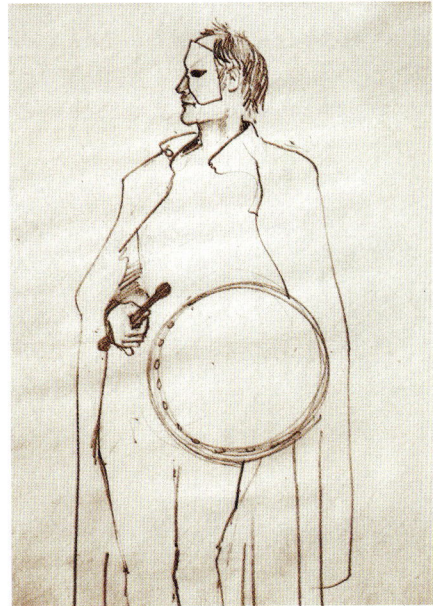

Sketch of Simon with bodhrán drum

95

I noticed that some of the physical characteristics of the people we saw around town began to creep into the portrayals of the Shakespearean parts the actors were playing.

The Duke of Gloucester, for example, played by Joe, had a definite stoop and his hands were often clasped behind his back. It was weird to be there in the grounds of a psychiatric hospital creating a play that embodied themes of madness.

In the end, when the play was up and running, you wouldn't have said the actors' characterisations were those of insane people. Not at all. Actors are very good at observing body language, and they were picking up gestures that would form any human tendencies. It's just that there were so many people at the hospital who were completely unguarded, whose frailties were not masked by the usual social conventions and whose movements were often exaggerated.

Two sketches for masks

The King Lear Poster

In the studio, I was painting an image for the poster to promote the *King Lear* show. I liked the scene in the play when Lear flees across the moors as a storm gathers, rending his clothes in a mad rage, berating the gods and provoking the storm to do its worst:

> *Blow, winds, and crack your cheeks! rage! blow!*
> *You cataracts and hurricanoes, spout*
> *Till you have drench'd our steeples, drown'd the cocks!*
> *You sulphurous and thought-executing fires,*
> *Vaunt-couriers to oak-cleaving thunderbolts,*
> *Singe my white head! And thou, all-shaking thunder,*
> *Smite flat the thick rotundity o' the world!*

It's a great speech, and what actor wouldn't relish doing it? Dave J as Lear made a great job of it, especially as he was about thirty years younger than the character he was portraying.

Around this time, I noticed an article in an Italian magazine about a strange abandoned garden at Bomarzo near Viterbo called the Garden of Monsters. Wonderful stone sculptures that adorned the garden in the late nineteenth century were slowly falling into decay. One of them was a giant head with a wide-open mouth, so big you could sit inside at a little stone table where the tongue would have been. I decided to fuse the two images and got to work painting a monolithic stone visage set against a stormy sky. Visible through the open mouth, a lightning bolt illuminated three distant figures in silhouette on the open moorland.

Feverishly trying to meet the deadline, I was up all night painting before the day it was due at the printer in Pontedera. After hours of silence, lost in my own world, the street door burst open and a man lurched into the studio, scaring the life out of me. I ventured a nervous smile, guessing it was a patient from the hospital on his way

Photo taken in the Bomarzo Garden of Monsters, Viterbo near Rome

back before curfew, as it was after nine o'clock. He fixed one eye on me while the other looked off somewhere to the left at the wall. His gestures and lack of speech led me to guess that he was probably deaf and mute, which was fine by me because my Italian wasn't great.

After my heart had settled back in its cage I relaxed a bit, deciding that his demeanour was benign. His one good eye twinkled with a mischievous intelligence that was somehow gently disarming. I extended a rather bungling nonverbal welcome, and he came and stood beside me and gazed at the painting. He scrutinised the eye holes in the monolithic head, where I had painted a starburst behind one eye and a lunar eclipse through the other. The design was very intense in effect, and I shuddered to think what he would make of it. He screwed his index finger into his cheek, a gesture I'd often seen Italians use for a liking of something. I thanked him for the appreciation. He then pointed to the eyes while thrusting out a bottom lip and reinforced his dubious opinion with his right hand, which stretched out, palm down and rocked from side to side. He disappeared as abruptly as he'd arrived, flashing a smile of brilliant white teeth from his unshaven face at the doorway. And then he was gone.

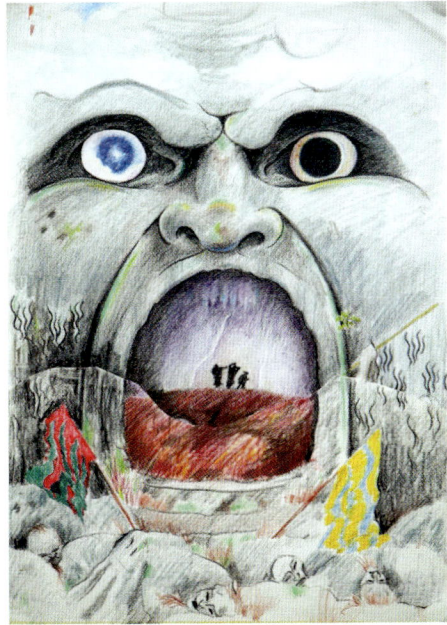

Sketch for King Lear poster

The silence crowded me, and I went out to smoke a cigarette and contemplate what had happened. Outside, the gathering darkness brought the fireflies out to play, blinking their magic lights under the acacia trees. After a few minutes in reverie, I went back to work.

At six in the morning I was adding finishing touches. Standing back one last time, I still felt troubled by the strange man's judgement. I decided to do a brief experiment, cutting out two bits of paper the exact shape and size of the eyes in the painting and then quickly sketched the cloud colours of the background sky onto them. I stuck them on to the painting, thus obliterating the starburst and lunar eclipse, and then I stood back.

All at once the great stone face turned into a gigantic mask. The viewer's attention is drawn in through the eyes to the heart of the storm and then straight down to the figures standing on the moors by the lightning striking the earth. It was bloody perfect. I was so excited I raced to the printers in the Fiat and fell asleep waiting for them to open the shop.

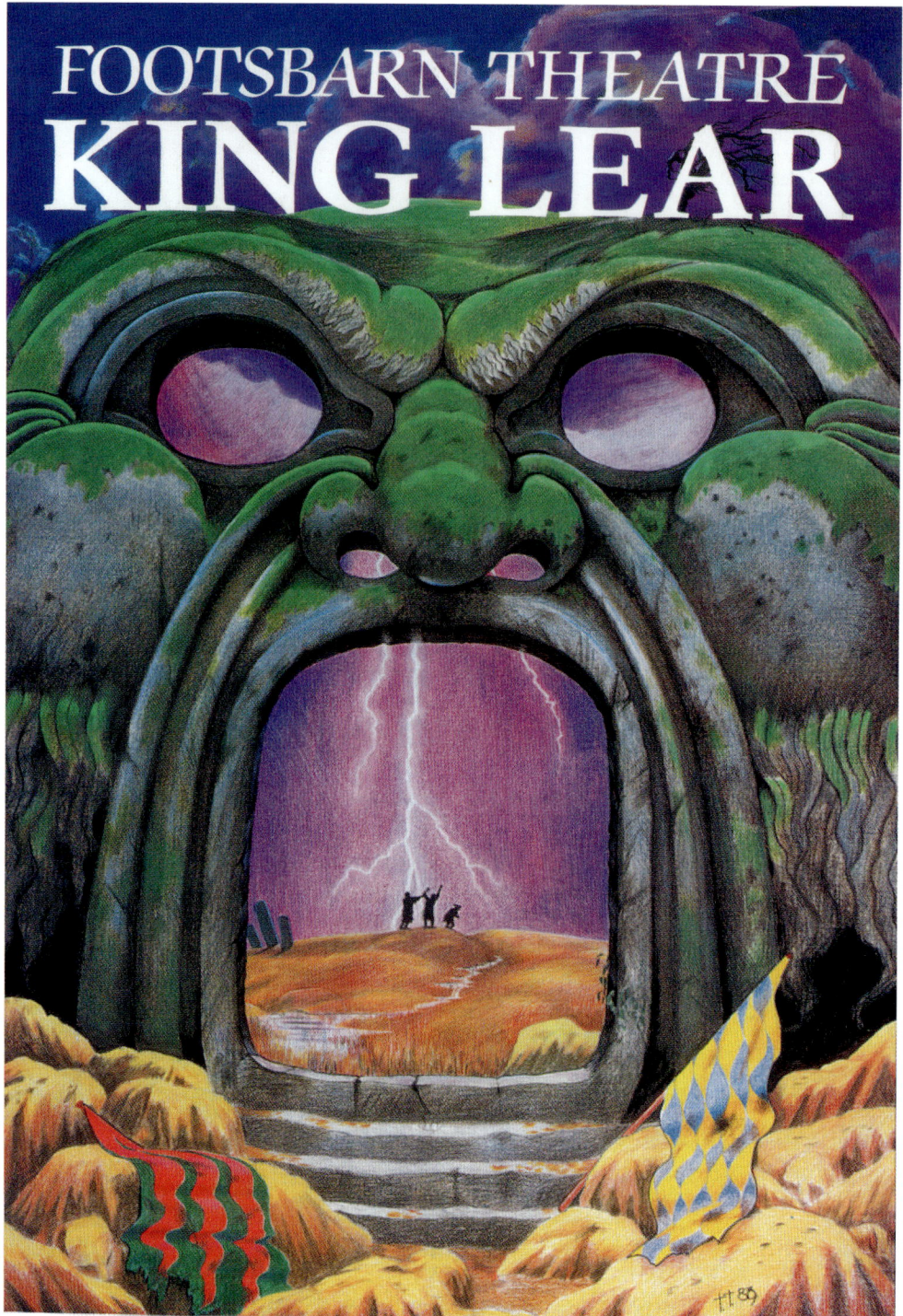

Final King Lear poster

The lesson learned was one that artists face all too often and find it hard to avoid falling into the trap. It is so easy to make things more complicated than they need to be, especially when you want to show off your skills. Simplicity is the best policy. Nature doesn't try to push rivers uphill if there is an easier way to reach the sea. The spectacular effects that I had put into the eyes were confusing and unnecessary, whereas the two scraps of paper with sketchy clouds scribbled on them brought the entire design together effortlessly.

Later that summer the poster was reproduced in billboard size by the Comune di Roma, who posted it all around Rome city centre. It was a proud moment, but I had to admit that it wasn't exactly *all* my own work. I silently thanked my mute friend from Volterra for the finishing touch.

The finished show with its stretched canvas set and cave-like entrances proved to be a worthy and very simple setting for the play. The masked chorus of musicians and flag bearers wore canvas capes that were singed and ripped in shreds in a similar fashion to the set behind them and at times, they blended to near invisibility. Margaret played Cordelia, the favourite of the King's daughters, with a bare face as well as one of the other daughters, Goneril, wearing a white mask with wolverine qualities. Maggie played the third daughter, Regan, wearing a birdlike white mask.

It is these two sisters and their conniving husbands who reduced the King's retinue from an army to a mere handful of loyal helpers. After their schemes have succeeded, Regan asks, 'What need one?' At this point, Lear reckons he's going mad and flees across the moors with only his Fool in tow.

Maggie, with the Regan's mask discarded, played the Fool who, as a foil for the King, is used to talking in riddles and nonsense. However, as the King's language shows more signs of madness, the Fool's utterances begin to make more sense.

King Lear, sitting on his chariot, rebukes Cordelia while the King of France and the Duke of Gloucester look on, dismayed

The King's throne, which was a perambulating contraption with two wheels at the front, turned into a careering obstacle with a tendency to lift off and fly during the famous storm scene. Simon's gongs struck up a suitably thunderous accompaniment to the hell breaking loose on stage. The ever helpful Edgar, who not only cares for the welfare of the King but saves his own father, Gloucester, from suicide by deceiving the now blind old man into believing he has indeed jumped off the cliffs of Dover and miraculously survived, when in reality he had only fallen a few feet.

The play offered plenty of opportunities for Footsbarn to show off their adept talent for mixing horror with benign emotions and humorous scenes. While Paddy, masked as the Duke of Cornwall, obviously relished the 'out vile jelly' scene when he poked Gloucester's eyes out, he was able to contrast that wickedness a few scenes later with the kindness of Edgar who he played with a bare face. Rod, playing the evil Edmund, this time without a mask,

Goneril and Lear as the storm approaches. Simon on the left is poised to launch an assault on those gongs and drums to create the almighty sound effects

likewise contrasted that character with his role as the loyal Kent who he played wearing a mask. So all the actors had numerous roles along with the musicians except for Dave, who played Lear throughout and was rarely off stage.

Oddly, one of the first *outdoor* performances after the initial opening at the University theatre in Asti, where the Italian theatre cognoscenti gave the production its blessing, the play had to be stopped half way through the show because of the imminent threat of a real storm which was rumbling directly overhead. As the audience headed for the car park, a young woman passing by me said to her partner, '*Non ho capito niente*' ('I didn't understand anything').

The rural audiences were obviously going to struggle with the Shakespearean English, but the play still proved popular when it settled into a rhythm and became a visual spectacle as much as anything with classically poetic leanings. While the actors enjoyed the spoken richness of the language, Footsbarn was never that 'high brow'.

Avignon and the Palais des Papes

When the show was ready and we went back on the road, we played at several festivals in open-air settings. When we presented *King Lear* at the Avignon Festival in France in July 1983, it was another opportunity to spend time with Els Comediants. This time I invited Ollie Jennings to come over from Galway so he could see their *Devils* show. He'd be able to see Footsbarn's *King Lear* as well, in case he wanted to bring it to the Galway Arts Festival the following year (which he did, in August 1984).

So Ollie arrived with Paraig Breathnach and the three of us went to the Palais des Papes in the centre of old Avignon to watch Comediants do this classic show. Although I'd seen it several times before, on this occasion it was particularly irreverent and shocking. Here

The Catalan group, Els Comediants, with
their Devils show

in the square in front of the Palace of the Popes, the impish devils were everywhere, even among the audience, who had stuffed the place to the gills. Overhead wires had been rigged with fireworks and Catherine wheels. The smell of incense and gunpowder mingled with red smoke.

The Comediants scaled the buildings and ran along the rooftops, while down below mythical creatures and huge dragons spat fire and belched smoke. It was an audacious invitation to us all to retake the Palace for the people. Not even the gold statue of the Virgin Mary high above

The spectacular Devils

us on the pinnacle of a tower could escape their clutches. It all came to a thrilling end with organ music roaring out of massive speakers. As the demons disappeared and the frenzy was slowly replaced with an eerie silence, people started to drift away.

Turning to my two friends, I asked them what they thought of it. Neither one said a word but just looked far away into the distance. I felt bad because I'd asked them to come all this way from Ireland, and now they didn't know what to say to me. It took me a while to realise that they were dumbstruck. Their minds were racing with possibilities, and after a few minutes they started talking. That show did go to Galway in 1985, and Galway was never the same again. In a summer that had spawned a spate of religious sightings of moving statues across Ireland, the arrival of Els Comediants with *The Devils* show was an exhilarating counterpoint. The possibilities that Ollie and Paraig conjured in their dreams led to the birth of Macnas, the company they developed in Galway that went on to lead the way in Irish street theatre.

Like all seminal moments, the impact these companies and performers had is locked into their time and era. Their influence is absorbed over time into the collective psyche. Els Comediants were born into an explosion of Catalan street culture that had been suppressed by Franco for decades. They wanted to embrace a modern culture that could infuse myth, ritual and the arts and folk crafts that would bring people together to celebrate. *The Devils* was just one of their shows, but it obviously touched an international nerve. In the Irish context, you have to look at the issues the country faced in those times. The manacles of society's collaboration with church and state were about to come off. Macnas, just like *Riverdance* years later, would tap into a rich vein of Celtic myth and legend and deliver a culturally vibrant product pumped with twentieth century steroids, full of music and dance and everything that would appeal to baby boomers brought up on rock and roll.

It proved that you didn't have to hang out in the capital cities of Europe to be a mover and shaker. Footsbarn were from Cornwall, Comediants were from Canet de Mar and Macnas were based in the west of Ireland, the very fringes of the continent. Fringe theatre was enjoying a hiatus in Edinburgh, Avignon and many other European festivals. If you could showcase your work here and succeed, then you could watch the effects rippling across the continent. And that is also one of the great things about festivals. It's not just a feast of different shows within a short time and space; it's a coming together whereby audiences, performers, directors and producers can mingle, share ideas and take them back across the world. Movies can do a lot of things, but no movie can give you an experience like the night in the Palais des Papes. It's theatre of the senses, and you have to be *in it*.

Post-performance pizza party, France

After the party was over in Avignon, which included a hot Sunday afternoon by the river, half in, half out and half naked with all the performers and dignitaries, we had a brief sojourn to do *King Lear* for one night at the gorgeously named open-air Roman arena at Sophia Antipolis. Eric Idle (of Monty Python fame) graced us with his presence, accompanied by his wife, Tania Kosevich. Eric chatted with the actors at the bar after the show while I talked to Tania at a separate table. He looked across at us from time to time and eyed me with some suspicion. I'm not surprised, because Tania was a professional model, strikingly beautiful and absolutely charming. We chatted away through the evening until it ended in the small hours of the following morning and, without hesitation, Eric paid the entire bar bill – no mean gesture considering the way Footsbarn folk could drink!

We didn't see many celebrities during my time with Footies. Friends and family often turned up in the strangest places, but meeting the likes of Eric Idle was rare. At a one-night stand in Boulder, Colorado, in 1982, Allen Ginsberg came on stage reciting his poetry to the strains of our *Rockin' Tossers* music and cabaret show. It was a bit weird but nice of him to join us. Once, when I was at my printers, I was introduced to the Polish actor Ryszard Cieslak, whose mentor, the great Polish theatre director Jerzy Grotowski, was setting up his Workcentre right there in Pontedera. Grotowski had published a book in 1968, *Towards a Poor Theatre*, as a result of his experimental theatre in Poland, and his work influenced training and techniques across the world, not least among some of our own actors. I'm afraid to admit that Ryszard Cieslak's importance was lost on me at the time. Not that I made a fool of myself or anything; it's just that if our actors had been there they probably would have kissed his feet. Sadly, he died only a few years later while teaching in Houston. Grotowski went on teaching almost in secret in Pontedera until 1999.

People were drawn to Footsbarn from all walks of life. One of our greatest fans at the time was the wife of the British ambassador to France. She invited us to lunch one time at an incredible apartment on the Île de la Cité, right in the heart of Paris with a view across the Seine. An exuberant and eccentric woman, she was an excellent host and didn't seem to mind that these ragamuffins were about to devour and drink everything that the kitchen and the cellar could provide. It remains one of the great lunches of my life. On the opposite side of the coin, a Swiss guy called Marco turned up several times in Portugal, and then weirdly he popped up again in Denver and Santa Fe, saying he was buying horses in Wyoming. He was later arrested in Portugal by Interpol for an armed bank robbery in Switzerland, and that got the rest of us in deep shit. It was especially tough for those of us who had bought rural smallholdings near Baranco and Milfontes, because the local newspapers associated this guy with us, even though we knew nothing about him or his background.

Pisa

In August it was back to Italy. Ollie came with me in the Fiat, and Paul was in the back. I was in a hurry to get to Pisa so that I could surprise Ollie by arriving at the Leaning Tower in the dead of night. It must have been around one o'clock in the morning when I drove into the piazza where the tower and cathedral reside in splendour. There would have been a hushed silence but for a car full of young lads from Milan arriving at the same time, who spilled out on the lawn laughing and whooping at what they saw. While Ollie and Paul stood in amazement and rubbed the sleep out of their eyes, I joined the boys from Milan who were already doing cartwheels in sheer delight.

During the day this spot is crowded with tourists and sightseers. It is probably one of the most photographed buildings in the world, and there is no doubting its status as a wonder. But at night, when there is no one around, it is even more bizarre, with the greenish light that illuminates the tower giving it an almost alien quality. It's as if the gods had thrown some kind of ancient prototype rocket from the heavens and landed it in Pisa, nose first with the rest sticking out at an angle.

In 1983 you could scramble all over the tower during opening hours, as there wasn't so much as a guard rail to stop you, even between the columns on the upper ledges. It's not surprising that Galileo thought about doing experiments with gravity at the Leaning Tower. You only have to walk up the three hundred steps that spiral the inside tower walls to feel its primal force. This is because it pitches you into a clown routine: you can easily break into a trot on the side of the building that leans, but then struggle and puff against gravity up the steps on the opposite side. This act goes on and on, round and round, making you feel very silly until you get to the top.

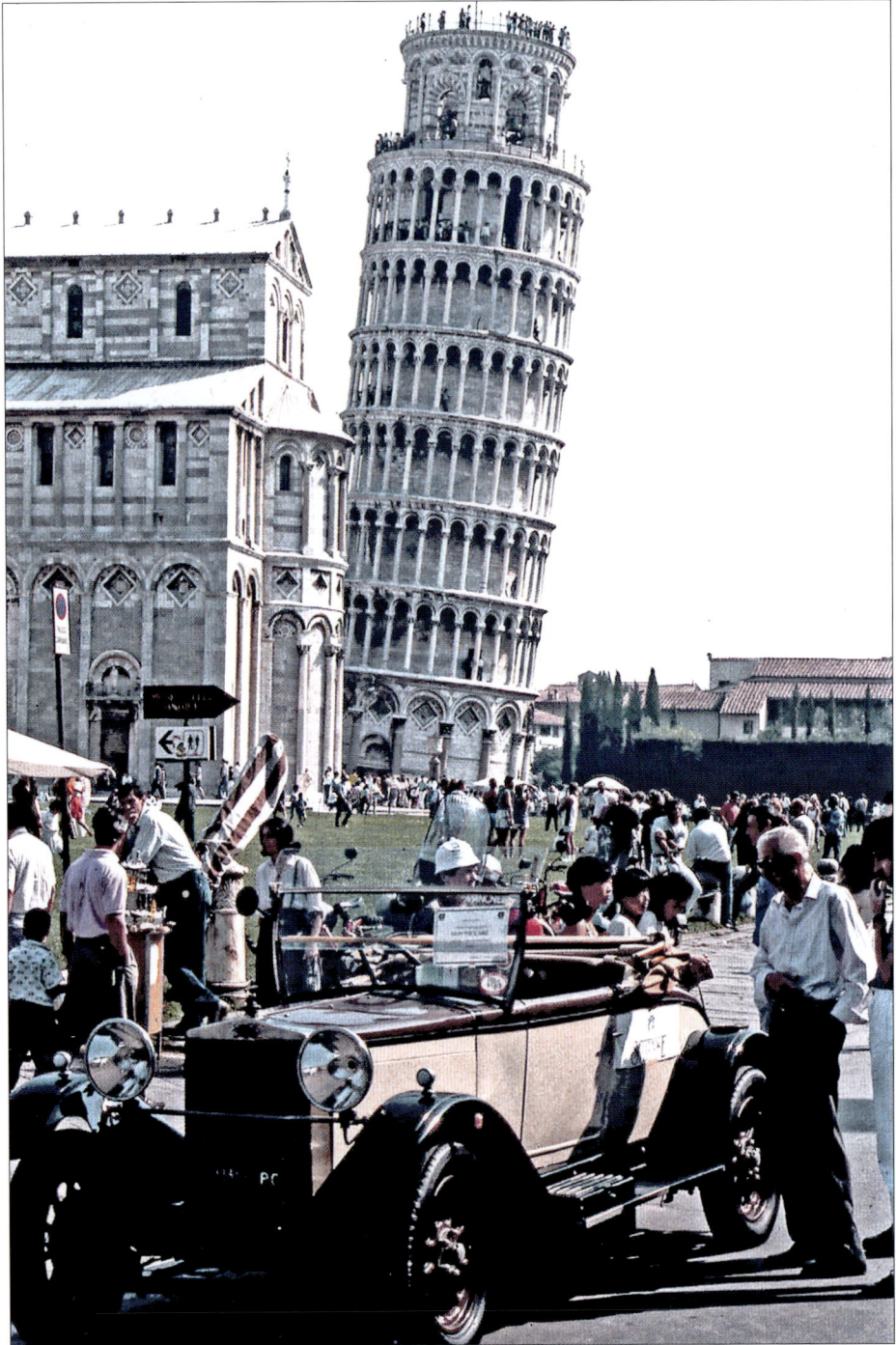

Leaning Tower of Pisa thronged with tourists by day

From there, if you're not too dizzy, you can enjoy the magnificent scene. The symbols of the wealthy past lie before you, including the cathedral and baptistry alongside it, with its wedding-cake architecture built from gorgeous white marble.

That night we stayed in Pisa, and because we were so late getting there the only hotel open was expensive. But it was a real treat. In the morning, I knocked on Ollie's door and said I was going down to breakfast and not to worry, I was paying. 'No, you're not!' came a shout from inside, but it was too late, and besides, he was only half dressed and couldn't follow me down the great swirling staircase that led to the foyer. He dashed back into the room and emerged again with thousands of lire in paper money, which he threw into the open space in the middle. As I took to the bannisters for extra speed, Ollie's experiment with gravity was thwarted by air resistance, so as I reached the bottom and disappeared into the lobby, dozens of notes floated softly to the ground floor tiles after me. Bed and breakfast on me was a small gesture of repayment for the years of generous hospitality he'd given me in Galway.

Familiarity with nudity was a recurring theme in Italy and something that the Italians seemed to be at ease with, more than most other cultures I'd experienced before. Of course, you can't walk far in Rome without bumping into sculptures of naked men and women in public fountains. The one in Piazza Barberini is particularly sexy but for the traffic whizzing round it. Even the state television station, RAI, closed down each night with an elegant solo female striptease. Well, there wasn't much tease, because it usually ended with the full Monte Carlo. I showed Ollie when he got up to switch off the TV. I said, 'No, wait till you see this.' He nearly coughed his teeth out. We laughed at the thought of RTÉ in Ireland trying to do that.

Lucia

Florence was great but very hot in August because it sits in a saucer-shaped basin with the Arno river running through it. The hill towns are more airy and cool. However, finding a girlfriend for the first time in two years made everything more interesting. Lucia was working in Florence for the festival Il Paese dei Balocchi ('The Land of Toys', the island where Pinocchio lives). When we became friends, she was kind enough to show me around and translate important stuff I couldn't manage myself, especially when Italians spoke so fast.

Contrary to what you might be expecting, I didn't get to see Lucia naked because she said one of her breasts was smaller than the other (as if it mattered), so I had to make do with her bare back. This kept me entirely contented, as it reminded me of one of Picasso's blue-period paintings before he raided the African Art Museum and threw the contents at some women from Avignon. It came back to me again when I watched the movie *As Good As It Gets* and saw Greg Kinnear sketch Helen Hunt sitting on the edge of the bath with her back to him. The sight of Lucia's long, tapering torso, with a mass of black hair tumbling over her shoulders, was plenty for a poor boy starved of female intimacy for so long.

She was adorable and completely nuts, and when she smiled at me I melted like white chocolate in the sun. After several months in Italy I realised that she wasn't nuts at all and that her behaviour was normal for anyone brought up in this wonderful country. In the Italian way, she would suddenly erupt into a frenzy of dramatic gestures, with hands and arms waving about like a scarecrow in a storm, then deliver a verbal torrent in Italian that I only ever half understood. When she left to go home to Palermo at the end of the season in Rome and it was time for Footsbarn to go back to France, she said:

'You can never come to visit me in Sicily, Ted.'

'Why is that, Lucia?'

'Because my brothers would kill you!'

Florence was the only place I ever lost my wallet. I was on my own in the Luna Park one lunchtime, looking across the river and eating a sandwich, when a woman who must have been eighty sat by me with her little dog. She kept reaching down to pet the dog and, of course, I didn't realise what she was up to until I was at a cafe some hours later and the shoulder bag I'd had resting on the ground at the park bench was now missing the wallet.

But that pales as a memory compared to what Lucia pointed out to me late one night as we drove out of the same park. Among the bushes along the edges of the road near the entrance, a series of tableaux appeared out of the darkness. With their own little up-lit floodlights, probably run on battery systems, naked or semi-naked figures danced and waved to passersby. It was extraordinary because some of them were obviously men and some were cross-dressers, but it seemed that because of this, the women on show had to expose everything to prove what they weren't!

Lucia screeched with delight. 'Stop the car, Ted. Look at her, she is beautiful. Don't you want to go with her?' And she was beautiful, it was true. Every bit as beautiful as the Botticelli painting she was replicating as she swayed her hips slowly and curled the waist-length hair around her belly. Whether she was just exhibiting or touting for business I never found out, but on reflection, compared to anything the skin trade offers nowadays, this remains for me the most sublime, bizarre and tantalising vision of sex on show I've ever seen.

When we got back to Lucia's flat with a bottle of red wine, we couldn't find a bottle opener so in exasperation I placed the bottle on the tiled floor and pushed the cork into the bottle with my thumb. It would go only so far and then bob back up again. With one last, forceful effort the entire bottle exploded, sending shards of glass and red liquid everywhere. I looked at my hands, trying to recover my shocked senses. What was wine and what was blood? With relief I slowly realised it was all wine. I had one tiny sliver of glass in my wrist. How much worse it could have been doesn't bear thinking about. We cleaned up the mess, and I thanked my lucky stars and didn't bother about lamenting the loss of wine. Stupid boy!

Our shows for that festival involved a hastily improvised spectacle with large puppets for the Botanical Gardens one Sunday afternoon as a free, open-air show for families, with more shows after dark. I had been given the task of procuring fireworks. Me? Fireworks? Okaaay . . . An advertisement in the local directory led me to a family of gypsies making their own fireworks in a remote farmhouse in the Arno valley. Having got myself lost several times, I eventually stumbled on the place with long, low sheds on the horizon. Dogs on chains were attached to long wires so they could snap and bark at you all the way up the drive but never get close enough to bite. At least, that was my trusting assessment.

At the door, I was greeted by a group of girls probably ranging from eighteen into the early twenties, with tanned skin and black eyes and even darker fingernails, whose tirade of questions in an unfamiliar dialect sent me into a shocked silence and made me wonder whether talking to the dogs might be a better option. When their father appeared and I had recovered my composure, we got down to the business in hand. The girls, who were making fireworks with all kinds of different powders, continued to flirt and tease me mercilessly in the background. Every attempt at questions I made in my pathetic Italian set them off giggling. After an hour of this embarrassing torture, I was relieved to come away with a ton of fireworks – though I had only the slimmest idea of which ones went bang and which went aahhh with lovely colours.

Fortunately, our technician, Dave H, was so impressed he sent me back for more after the first show, as he'd used up most of the fireworks and no one had got burned. Returning to face the gypsy girls a second time, I was ready for their saucy cheek and I enjoyed the banter. This time they were slightly more respectful, if no less flirtatious, and any wink or clown-like gesture I made set them off again in hysterics. Their black fingers instinctively tried to hide their giggling faces, which only resulted in sooty smears across their cheeks and noses. I do hope they are still alive, because whatever they were doing, it wasn't kosher with health and safety regulations.

I had to do advance publicity in Rome, so while the rest of the gang took a two-week holiday, Lucia and I camped in one of our trucks in Villa Borghese, a huge park in the centre of Rome. It was an extraordinary privilege to have one's travelling office in such sump-tuous surroundings at the Parco dei Daini, the open-air theatre where we were going to set up. It was also next to the zoo, so the sound of exotic bird calls and wild animals made it all the more bizarre.

It was here, on the temporary stage we were going to use the fol-lowing week, that I saw Maguy Marin's dance company performing *May B*, inspired by Sam Beckett's work. I had never seen anything like it. It was as if the inmates of the asylum had taken over the dance and movement class. That sounds like it was mad, but we were taken on a deeply human emotional ride. We laughed at their antics, wept with their despair, marvelled at the synchronised dance moves and strangely identified with the individual lost souls. I so wanted to get this show to the Galway Arts Festival, but I failed on that score; *May B* didn't make it to Ireland until it was revived and appeared at festivals in Enniskillen and then Dublin thirty-eight years after that night in Rome.

BY THE TIME OUR COMPANY ARRIVED in Rome to start the shows, I already knew my way around and felt at home on Via Veneto, the street that lent its name to the movie and the phrase *Dolce Vita*. Sad-ly, as it was now October and the nights were getting cold, it was the last of our outdoor gigs for that year and time for Lucia and I to go our separate ways. She went south to Palermo, and I headed north for the Alps and onwards to a new base camp in France. I never saw her again, but a couple of years later I was told by letter from a friend in Galway that a girl working with Els Comediants had been asking for me. I assumed it was one of the Spanish girls in the company and thought how sweet that they remembered me. I was in Australia at the time, still working with Footsbarn, so I missed Comediants' visit to Galway in the summer of 1985. I found out thirty years later that it was Lucia who had been asking for me.

I pined all the way to France in the Fiat 124, playing music on my Sony Walkman and singing 'On Days Like These', trying to sound like Matt Monro in *The Italian Job* as I climbed into the Alps. The car was Italian registered, with Pisa plates. It was an old banger, really, but sitting behind the wheel it was easy to pretend that I was driving a Lamborghini. Okay, so maybe that was a bit of a stretch of the imagination, but it had been an asset in Rome when I learned to drive the proper Italian way. It was like being in a video game all the time, and if you didn't do as the Romans did, you were lost – game over.

As an introvert I had to let go of my inhibitions, learning to use hand gestures and screaming out of the open window to insult any driver who cut across me at a junction without stopping or even looking. Then I'd do the same to some other sucker, who'd be left in a cloud of dust because he was too slow off the blocks. It all worked, er, erratically and it was fun while I was in Rome. But it was a different story when I found myself facing the wrong way in the fast lane of the motorway near Carrara, having aquaplaned on a sheet of water in torrential rain and spun the car round three times. In a blind panic to get the car restarted before the oncoming traffic ploughed into me, it took a few seconds to realise that there wasn't another vehicle in sight, either in front or coming up behind me. It was a miraculous escape. I calmly got the car facing in the right direction and headed north, telling the boy racer inside me to get out and go back to Rome. I took it easy after that. '*Questi giorni quando vieni, il bel sole.*' On days like these, la la la la, la-la la-la.

By the time I got to Col de Montgenèvre, one of the high Alpine passes on the border with France, it was already dark. The Italian customs officials were quite serious when they told me I couldn't take an Italian-registered car out of the country if I didn't have an Italian address.

Furthermore, they suspected that my UK driving licence – which was mostly in Welsh and still had my parents' address on it – was a fake, because it didn't expire until 2020. This was 1983. If I wanted to go off to France, I would have to get official permission or prove where in Italy the car was licensed. Bureaucracy is the plague of southern Europe. It's never enough to have the right document. For example, the conversation below was typical in Italy, and could just as easily occur in Portugal or Spain:

'I'm afraid you haven't got your document stamped, sir.'

'Oh. Where do I get that done?'

'The municipal offices. But you will need to get stamps first.'

'Oh. I have to buy stamps? Where do I get stamps?'

'The tobacconist downtown. But he's closed for siesta. He opens again at four o'clock.'

'Right. What time do the municipal offices close?'

'Four o'clock.'

'Grazie, signore. See you tomorrow, then.'

'Prego.'

It was always a nightmare. Wasn't the book *Catch-22* set in Italy? I think it was.

I spent the night in the albergo right there by the customs post sleeping fitfully, wondering how I was going to get out of this mess. When I got up the following morning, the police seemed to be in better spirits and they gestured for me to go. 'Vai a Francia. Go on, get out of here.'

Bless the little Fiat, it always started first time, except for this cold, blue, high-altitude October morning. This set them off chuckling, sticking their thumbs behind their waistline belts, and then, with hats removed, they mopped their brows with great white handkerchiefs, one elbowing the other and gesturing for the rest to come out of the office so they could all enjoy this new blood sport. I could feel myself getting smaller and smaller until I could hardly see over the dashboard. Come on, you bastard, start! Suddenly, the senior officer was at the window wagging his finger. Wait! Oh, please! The steep hill the car was parked on might just come to the rescue. All I needed was a bit of help turning the car around, and I could jump-start it down the hill.

'No, no, finito adesso.' His serious face had returned. He then used a word which sounded awfully like 'confiscate'. Maybe they had been having a bit of fun. Maybe they'd removed the leads of the distributor under the bonnet during the night. That seemed unlikely. Maybe they were waiting for a wad of lire in a brown envelope (as if I had any Italian money left to give them). I'll never know. I waited for one of our trucks to come through so I could empty the car of its contents. Simon came along in his new truck, and we said goodbye to the Fiat 124. It was probably the worst thing I ever did for Footsbarn. I lost the bloody company car!

A Home in France

In spite of this last encounter with Italians at the border, I really missed Italy when we settled at the new base in France. I had advocated having a base in Tuscany, but I had to concede that it made much more sense to have a home in France. Monsieur and Madame Roux's generous offer of their old farmhouse at Saint-Siffret near Uzès in the south of France was perfect. Besides, the French government was very supportive of the arts and wanted to make France an example to the world. It was obvious that we would do well touring theatres in France, as we did eventually, without a tent, in a streamlined version of the company with just one truck and a bus.

John watching a show from the sidelines in Uzés

Joe taking a photo of me taking a photo of the Pont du Gard,
close to the base camp at Saint-Siffret, Uzés

Our stay in Saint-Siffret was very civilised compared to the situation we'd left behind in Spain only twelve months previously. On a visit home for Christmas this time, I was able to buy a decent bottle of wine in Warrington on my way to see my parents in Wales. I'd forgotten the lingo from years spent abroad. The girl in the off-licence said, 'Jer wonit wrappin, or wot?' Welcome back to Blighty, Ted.

And if you think that is snobby, you'd be right. By the time I returned to France in the new year, I thought I was the bee's knees, listening to Simple Minds' *New Gold Dream* tape on a new Walkman, and wearing an expensive, soft wool navy bomber jacket from Paris with racing green sleeves that zipped out at the shoulder and a bright red contrasting lining. I had a ticket for the TGV that was going to whisk me to Avignon at 240 kilometres an hour. *And* I was returning to my own room in a lovely old house on an asparagus farm in the south of France. I was blissed out! I bought a second-hand caravan from a very nice French gendarme who told me it was as strong as an ox, and he was right. Compare all this to the life of yesteryear, erecting my little tent in all weathers every time we stopped, or sleeping in the cab of the truck, and you can appreciate the difference the new lifestyle made.

Charmian and Rod's wedding in the new tent

The spring of 1984 was a lot of fun for us all. At the end of February we did a parade on a crisp but sunny day for the carnival in the local village, only a couple of

Paddy, Rod, Steve and Pete at the wedding party

weeks after the region had been turned white overnight with half a metre of snow. A new theatre tent was ordered from England, all creamy-white new canvas, and it was christened with Rod and Charmian's wedding in Saint-Siffret before we went back on the road with the new show, our version of Brecht's *Caucasian Chalk Circle* which we called *Chinese Puzzle*. We created and rehearsed the show in France during the first few months of the year.

The story begins with a dispute arising within a travelling circus troupe not unlike Footsbarn itself, and is resolved by the telling of the Chalk Circle judgement similar to that of

Joe on bass

Sketches for Chinese Puzzle

King Solomon's in the Bible (Kings 3:16-18) wherein two women claim to be the rightful mother of a child. The story within the story then takes off on a wild ride involving dastardly Chinese authoritarian characters and winsome peasantry.

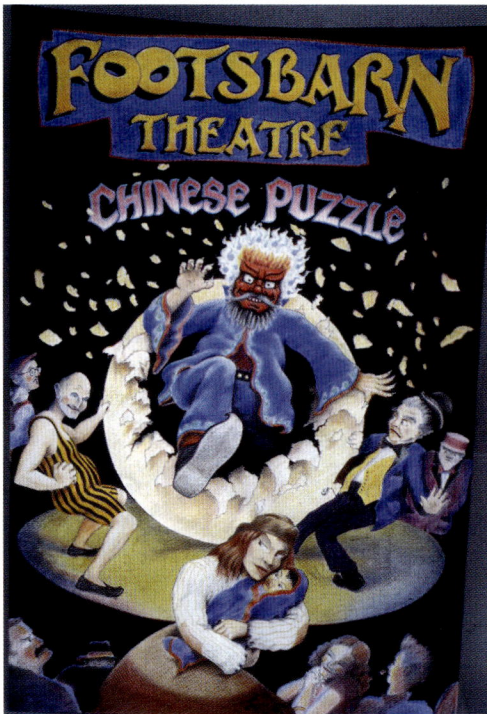

Finished poster for Chinese Puzzle

There was plenty of scope for the actors to play multiple roles and to don different masks and costumes in order to complete the line up of characters. Black-shirt henchmen terrorised everyone and insisted on inspecting your 'papers'. You could boo and hiss from the safety of an audience seat but those in the front row who couldn't show the right 'papers' were in danger of being ejected. Margaret, who played the central character and mother

Chinese Puzzle show with Pureza, Paul, Margaret, Maggie and Steve

Margaret pleading her case as the mother while the child
(with Pureza behind the mask) awaits her fate.

*Maggie, Joe as the judge and Margaret in the
final scene of Chinese Puzzle*

of the infant, had the audience on side within minutes, and thus we eagerly followed her progress during a good old fashioned chase and championed her fate all the way to the final courtroom judgement.

Unlike *Arthur*, *Hamlet* and *King Lear*, this show had a happy ending and its storyline appealed to women, naturally. It was reflected in the poster sales at front of house where, invariably, women would go for the *Chinese Puzzle* poster even if they'd actually seen one of the other shows.

By the end of March the new tent was delivered in an ex-removals truck, a good old British Bedford that happily towed my caravan, as I was going to be the one driving it. It was with this rig, driving along a German autobahn one lovely Saturday afternoon that coming summer, that I was pulled over by the German police, who issued a hefty fine and ordered me off the highway onto the minor roads. Asked for an explanation, they said I should have known that you can't take a vehicle towing a trailer of any kind on certain sections of the autobahn on certain weekends during certain months of the year when traffic is heavy. In any case, I was going too slow. Worse than this minor humiliation was that they sent a duplicate of the offence to the address on my Welsh driving licence. This caused great consternation when the letter landed on the hall tiles at my parents' house. My dad took the letter to his sister, who often took holidays in Germany, to see if she might be able to make sense of it. When she translated it she assumed that I'd been thrown in jail!

It took some days and much hand-wringing before they finally managed to contact me, and when I eventually talked to my mother on the phone, I said, 'Oh, that. Did the police send you something? Don't worry, I just had to pay a fine. So how are you?'

ANYWAY, IT WAS EARLY MAY BEFORE WE got everything ready to go touring again. The Johnston brothers were reunited after Steve joined us again, after a three-year absence, as an actor and musician. We had new technicians from England, Spencer along with Angela and their kids, Carlie and Nico, travelling in a gorgeous converted

A new truck to drive.
'It had to be better than The Brute.'

bus, Mick also from England, and Frenchman Bruno. After a stop in Aurillac to run-in the show, we were off crossing borders again. The festival in Zurich was brilliant. I liked its director, Jorge, a lot. He made sure we got a prime spot in a verdant park, right on the lake shore. The other performing artists were really cool, so it was an enjoyable gig. What surprised me was the number of bank employees who spilled out of the dozens of banks in the city and came down to eat a picnic lunch and sunbathe right in front of our camp. Maybe we were encroaching on their usual patch, but it didn't seem to bother them. The formal clothes for work all came off for half an hour. I wouldn't have thought that Swiss people were so uninhibited. Lunched out, lakeside and topless at 1.30 pm, back to bank-smart clerk by two o'clock. Els Comediants were here setting up their show on a little island close to shore. Both companies were in much demand by festivals so it was no wonder we kept crossing paths.

Back in Galway

By midsummer I was looking forward to going back to Galway with the company, not least because I could do business and talk to people in English. I was also looking forward to introducing Footsbarn to loads of friends, which turned out to be totally unnecessary – Footies already had dozens of friends of their own in Galway, so everyone dined out with their pals or entertained them on site. It was the third time Footsbarn had set up on Fisheries Field, and everyone loved it. This field was gaining a reputation for being one of the best tent sites in Europe. Surrounded on three sides by water, it was perfect for security. Highly visible from one of the major river crossings at the salmon weir, it was a beacon for publicity. The adjacent cathedral provided ample parking. It was perfect, and it still is. It was a lovely summer that year in Galway. The hay had been saved, and harvesting wheat and barley was well under way. This kind of weather was a blessing when working with a tent in Ireland. We experienced what adverse weather could be like two years later, in August 1986, when we were back in Galway with *Macbeth* and thankfully indoors at the Leisureland complex, because the lashing wind and rain blew people off the Prom in Salthill.

If I was slowly becoming more European as I entered my fourth year with Footsbarn, I knew my home was really in Galway and that if I ever got homesick, it was never for England, where I'd spent the school years of my life. No, it was for Ireland in general and Galway in particular. This might seem strange, because most Irish people who spend any time abroad, including those who emigrate completely, always refer to Ireland as 'home'. I never had the same feeling about *my* native land. I felt more at home in Wales, where I had spent my childhood summers with my aunt. There were lots of things I liked about England and the English, and if you turn me upside-down you'll find 'Made in England' stamped on the bottom, but I never felt I was at my natural best there. It wasn't a case of an

Footsbarn promoting the shows at the Galway Races

unhappy childhood or hopelessness at school; it was just a feeling when I first went to visit Ireland in 1973, that even with no known family ancestry, I felt completely at ease there.

Now, after decades as an artist in Galway and married to an American, I like to think that I am one of Galway's best-tolerated Englishmen. I am often asked by English and American people what it is about the Irish that makes them so friendly and so well liked around the world. I usually say two things. First of all, they remember your name even if they have only heard you say it once. Secondly, they have an extraordinary knack of asking questions without appearing to be nosey, and it's this 'art', if you like, that makes all the difference. I know many English people who are enormous fun – and many Americans too, some of whom would tell you their life story if you met them on the bus. But it's that ease of making you feel you're more important than they are themselves, that's where the Irish have you. It's very flattering and their interest in you is usually genuine.

I grew up an oddball artist: even as a child I liked the character Queequeg in the movie *Moby Dick*, who said to Ishmael, 'Can you read words? That's good, because I read pictures.' I was a quiet child who observed everything and spoke little. I read pictures. I wasn't interested in books without pictures or photographs in them. At art college I told jokes all the time and tried to be a funny man. I became socially adept and comfortable in company after I moved to Ireland and started picking up the cues from the way the Irish speak to one another. I am still amazed at how talented some Irish people are with the English language, as if poetry came naturally to them; they can make the rest of us seem like we can only manage to speak in tweets. I suspect that talent comes from a general pool that all Irish people dip into, because the culture is rich with the love of music and language just as, for example, Italians are steeped in visual beauty from a love of painting.

Saying goodbye to my Irish friends again was sad, but I was looking forward to a few days off by the banks of the River Loire in France before moving on to Lausanne in Switzerland. Joe, Steve H, Bruno and I set up camp by the riverside with only green fields in view. It was idyllic.

Some French girls came down to the river to swim in the afternoons, mercilessly flirting with the four of us. Joe called them the nubiles. On the third day, the nubiles came with their mother, who invited us to dinner at their house. Footies were never shy of an invitation to eat and drink, so the offer was gratefully accepted.

We attempted to smarten up a bit and did a reasonable job of making ourselves presentable, while the girls, back on home territory, had completely changed their spots! The cat women had turned into kittens, reverting in their neat uniforms to the schoolgirls they still were. Not that it mattered a jot. Papa was enjoying his role as master of ceremonies, and the girls ('*Oui, Papa.*' '*Non, Papa.*' '*Ça va, Papa, merci*') were on their best behaviour. Papa took centre stage with a bottle of champagne from the fridge. Taking an enormous sword off the wall over the mantelpiece, he gently tapped its edge around the neck of the bottle, and with a flourish of the blade, whoosh, he sliced the top of the bottle clean off. The champagne flowed and we all cheered. *Bon appétit, tout le monde!* I could have done with this guy's sword back at Lucia's flat in Florence when we were stuck for a corkscrew.

The site for our stay in Lausanne was a truly beautiful park, high on the hill overlooking the city and the lake. There were no showers on site, but we were told we could use the local shelter. Everything was shipshape, as you'd expect from the Swiss. What they neglected to explain was that by 'shelter' they meant the nearest nuclear fallout shelter. This was a ten-minute walk down the hill between two bungalows – or at least, the entrance was. Here a sloped ramp led down to what looked like an underground garage.

I was alone, which might not have been the best idea, but I was going for a shower, after all. I had a key. It worked easily, and if the door was heavier than normal, it swung open without fuss and I closed it behind me. A dimly lit corridor stretched out to infinity, and after what seemed like a very long walk, another door came into view. That too opened with the same key and closed behind me. After a third door and yet another corridor, I felt like I was somewhere deep under Mont Blanc. I wasn't normally claustrophobic, so this new feeling that was creeping over me was getting scary.

Eventually reaching something resembling a room was comforting, but then all the instructions posted around the walls on how to survive in this place for a year were terrifying. I thought, Jeez, give me oblivion every time! I'd prefer a stopover in Hades compared to this. The amount of canned food could have fed an army. Apparently it was sold off every year to poorer countries and restocked. I did manage to get a shower, and it was very efficient and not unpleasant, but the whole time, I couldn't help thinking completely irrational notions: Would anyone ever find me if the doors jammed? Would they discover a petrified body on the floor in a year or so when it was time to restock because I couldn't find a tin opener? I whistled with an air of bravado all the way back out of the mountain, and by the time I got to open air again I was drenched in sweat and needed to go back for another shower. No way! That would have to do for a few days, or maybe a week.

I was reminded of this two years later when we were in Salzburg, Austria, just after the Chernobyl accident happened. People were telling children not to eat berries or anything growing outside because it was contaminated. 'Well, it means they are covered with something, like poison, only you can't see it.' What a nightmare! I thought longingly about the Lausanne bunker under the Alps and wondered if I still had the key, long forgotten in the lining of my jacket or somewhere.

It was around this time when we were doing shows in Amsterdam that we had a visit from David Blenkinsop, director of the Festival of Perth in Australia. He not only offered us an invitation to

Perth but insisted that he could organise a tour of the entire country for us, supplied with a new tent and our own Australian vehicles. It was such an audacious idea but it was so far away! And could it really be done? The discussions about it went on for days, and then John's negotiations with the Festival of Perth and the Adelaide Festival, where it was proposed that we would present a new show created in Australia, went on for weeks. Meanwhile, summer was coming to an end, and we still had a tour in France and Belgium to finish through the autumn months.

Julie

Everyone warned me about Julie. 'Stay well clear of her,' they said. 'You won't get a wink of sleep!' When I joined Footsbarn Theatre Company in 1981, Julie was away visiting her father in Amsterdam. A couple of months later, she caught up with us in the south of France, halfway up the Pyrenees in the medieval hill town of Foix. We set up our theatre tent next to an old chateau, and the trucks, buses and caravans fanned out over the surrounding park, making good use of the shade from enormous horse chestnut trees. Julie was just two years old back then and already had the reputation for being the loudest member of the company, particularly in the screaming and bawling department. So it was imperative that you pitched your tent or parked your caravan as far away as possible from Julie, who would be living with her mother, Margaret, in her caravan.

Like many a mischievous child, Julie's bark was worse than her bite. Actually, I found her a very engaging child, who responded well to a caring firmness: once she knew where the boundaries were, her behaviour was acceptable. At least, that was my experience. As the months turned to years and Footsbarn's tour roamed across Europe, all the children in the company became family to me.

They enjoyed an unconventional education, becoming street-wise and knowledgeable via direct experience of the world from a life growing up on the road. Theirs was an extraordinary upbringing by any standard, and any shortfall in the depth of their education compared to more settled children seemed to be compensated by a wisdom that comes from being at ease with nature, the big city, foreign cultures and food, and the needs of basic survival. At times we were so poor that we didn't know where tomorrow's breakfast would come from. At those times the children often joined their parents to busk and perform tricks in the street.

So Julie was well used to street performance by the time she was a toddler. She took part in an act with Daniel, her father, in which she sat on a kitchen chair while he lifted both chair and child into the air and balanced them with one chair leg on his chin, no hands. The resulting applause from the amazed audience was meat and drink to Julie, and she lapped it up, beaming back with the cutest look of a one-year-old, blue-eyed, blonde bombshell. She was used to being the centre of attention from an early age, but in spite of the warnings I grew fond of her, and though she could be a handful, she was also great fun.

My abiding memory of Julie is from a night in 1984 when she was about four. Footsbarn were billed to perform *King Lear* at the Théâtre de L'Est in Paris, which was a high-class gig for Footies at the time. This wasn't our own tent we were performing in. This was a proper Parisian theatre, with posh seats, and we were on our best behaviour. Julie's mother, Margaret, a beautiful German actress with a smile as wide as the Mississippi, was playing the part of Cordelia, the king's favourite daughter who falls out with him over his insistence that she partake in a ceremonial show of affection. Cordelia thinks it's a load of crap, protesting that the king knows damn well that she loves him. Banished from his sight, Cordelia retreats to the continent with the very nice king of France, leaving Lear to foist all state powers on his two remaining daughters, which he later regrets, because they drive him to the edge of madness.

On this particular Parisian night, with the house almost full, I was sitting at the back of the auditorium when I noticed Julie wandering down the centre aisle, thumb in mouth and trailing a small blanket. This wasn't normal, as the children were usually in bed by the time the evening show started, and most of them would have been back at the camp a few miles away. Julie had probably been asleep on a sofa with the theatre staff and had somehow sneaked out. I wasn't unduly worried as the kids were well used to seeing their parents on stage, and besides, the gory bit in the play when Gloucester gets his eyes poked out had long passed. I was about to go and grab her when she stopped halfway down the centre aisle, still staring at the stage, and then a kind woman made room for Julie to sit snuggled up beside her. While Julie fell asleep, I kept one eye on her and the other on the play, which was reaching its emotional final scenes. It was the moment when Cordelia made her final entrance, limp and lifeless in the arms of her distraught and remorseful father. As he carries the dead body towards the front of the stage, he pleads to the heavens, 'Why should a dog, a horse, a rat have life / and thou no breath at all?'

It was also the moment when Julie, caught in the confusion between waking and sleeping, recognised that it was her mother there in a state of helplessness. Filling those famous lungs full of air, she bellowed, 'Mummmmmeeeeee' with the energy of a force-nine gale. Like an army of soldiers brought to attention, the entire audience swung round and gaped at her in bewilderment.

Normal service was resumed remarkably swiftly, thanks to the speed of the usherettes, who flew to Julie's rescue and whisked her away. As they passed me by, Julie threw me a guilty glance and then her tongue stuck out in my direction, before she resumed an expression of baleful woe and milked the pampering attentions of the usherettes. 'Oh, mon petit chou-fleur!' one of them whispered.

To her credit, the dead Cordelia never batted an eye, and to *his* credit, Lear did not drop Cordelia on the stage floor, which might have turned the tragedy into a comedy. Consummate professionals, they continued as if nothing had happened. Margaret remembers the incident to this day. As for Julie – she's forty-something now and has children of her own. She still has a fine pair of lungs, acts in the theatre and sings in her own band, White Crocodile, based in Marseilles. Long may she continue to entertain the good people of France.

AFTER THE SHOWS IN PARIS, WE WERE ON our way to Belgium, specifically Tournai and Namur. I took photographs looking down on Namur to show how compact the site had to be sometimes, for the sake of security, when we were in the centre of a big city with all the trucks and buses encircling the camp, nose to tail, like a wagon train in the Wild West.

At the end of our Christmas holidays, I was in Devon staying with Jon B and Caroline, two former Footies who had left the company in December 1982. The snow came down in great silent gobs, filling the Devon lanes up to the hedge tops. Old England never looked so pretty, but it was back to work as soon as the new year dawned.

Even though the snowploughs were out, I still managed to get the truck stuck in deep snow drifts down a narrow

In a tight corner of downtown Namur, Belgium – urban sites had to be nose to tail for security and vehicles had to shield the tent from extraneous noise

lane. After hours shovelling snow like a maniac, I was able to get out to the main roads again, and I made it just in time for us to set up at the theatre in Euston the following day for the London Mime Festival gigs. After that, on the last day of January, we left the snow behind and flew out to Perth, Australia.

When we arrived it was about 37 degrees Celsius.

Western Australia, February 1985

We nearly didn't make it to Perth. Henry decided he'd had enough of the long-haul flight at some point after Bangkok. Had enough to drink, that is. Well, everyone was at it but he probably had more than the rest of us, by the look of him. He wasn't creating a scene or anything like that. No, he was very quietly determined to get out through the emergency exit at thirty thousand feet above the Indian Ocean. Henry was a strong young man with a fairly big frame, so it took four of us plus the stewards to get him to release his grip on the door lever. We eventually cajoled him back into his seat and strapped him in; he'd not spoken a word through the entire incident. I thought it best to keep an eye on him for a while, but I needn't have bothered: he just blinked a few times, nodded and then belched before dozing off, bless him. I bet he still says it wasn't him.

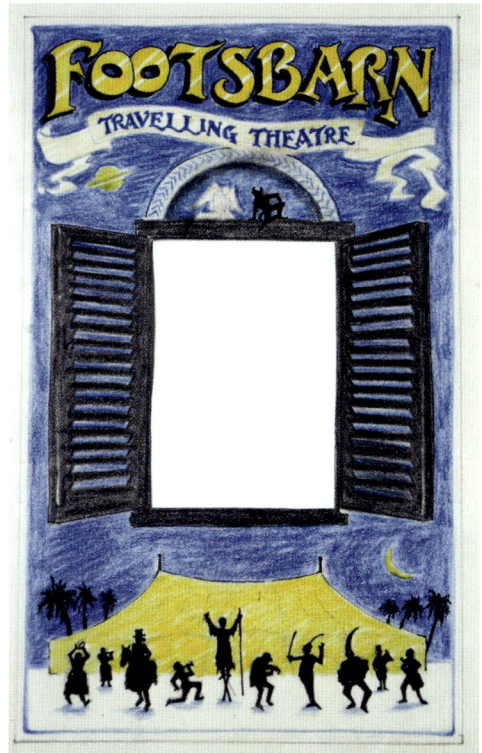

Poster sketch for tour of Oz 1985

135

Australia wasn't as popular as a destination back in the eighties as it is now. I'll come back to this subject later, but I should say at the outset that the nationwide tour ahead of us was going to be a totally new experience and on an unprecedented scale. So we needed to know a few things about the nature of Australia. First of all, the size of the place is similar to that of the United States, except that in Oz, most people cling to the coastal regions. Unless, of course, you're an Aboriginal person, in which case you can live anywhere because you have fifty thousand years of experience behind you. If you have ever seen the movie *Rabbit-Proof Fence* no doubt you marvelled at the two native girls who managed to evade the tracker to get home. What you can't get from the movie is the true sense of the distances those girls covered. They walked the equivalent of Galway to Moscow, mostly through the outback.

Yes, we were warned that there were venomous snakes and deadly spiders and some pretty nasty box jellyfish – in fact, some of the deadliest creatures in the world – but you've probably heard about those by now. We were also told that a kangaroo could give you a hell of a kick in the chest with its hind legs. But the worst danger we were going to face as we travelled all over the country was getting lost. So the first thing I did in Perth was buy a motorbike so I could go off into the bush whenever we stopped.

Australia was always a great sporting nation, as the success of the Sydney Olympics proved beyond doubt, but in the 1980s I think it was still suffering from the remnants of 'cultural cringe'. Not entirely confident with their own heritage, Australians were always looking to Europe for inspiration. Happily that has changed, and modern Australia is a confident nation with unique attributes. Australians are generally open-hearted people with a great capacity for fairness and honesty. I never had anything stolen in the whole sixteen months we were there.

They also have a great sense of humour, if sometimes a rather crass one. I came across a kiosk in a shopping mall in Noosa,

Queensland, where this tiny shop sold nothing but boxer shorts. It was called Strictly Ballroom, which I thought was pretty funny. Sometimes it could be shocking like the time I was at the enormous Melbourne Cricket Ground stadium watching Australia play India. It was very hot and the cricket was less than exciting. When a young woman carrying a tray of beers came up the aisle beside me, some Aussie wag in the crowd shouted, 'Show us yer tits!' The young woman put the tray down and lifted her tee shirt, revealing two very pleasantly formed breasts that she seemed rightly proud of. A huge cheer went up from thirty

Ted in Fremantle

or forty rows of seats around us, before she picked up the tray and went to join her friends, and normality resumed as if nothing had happened. I don't know if it still happens at the MCG but you certainly wouldn't get away with it at Lords.

On the darker side, I watched in horror one night soon after our arrival in Fremantle as two young women reeled out of a bar and fell into the gutter, screaming and fighting like mad dogs, while some guy followed them out, stood at the door, laughed, spat and went back inside. I turned to Joe and said, 'I think I must have lived a sheltered life.'

While trucks, buses, caravans and four-wheel-drive vehicles, some brand-new, were being collected for the tour that was about to begin, we opened with *King Lear* at the Perth Festival in our huge new theatre tent. I felt sorry for the actors and the audience because it was about forty degrees Celsius in there, so we rolled up the side walls of the tent to get the night air flowing through it.

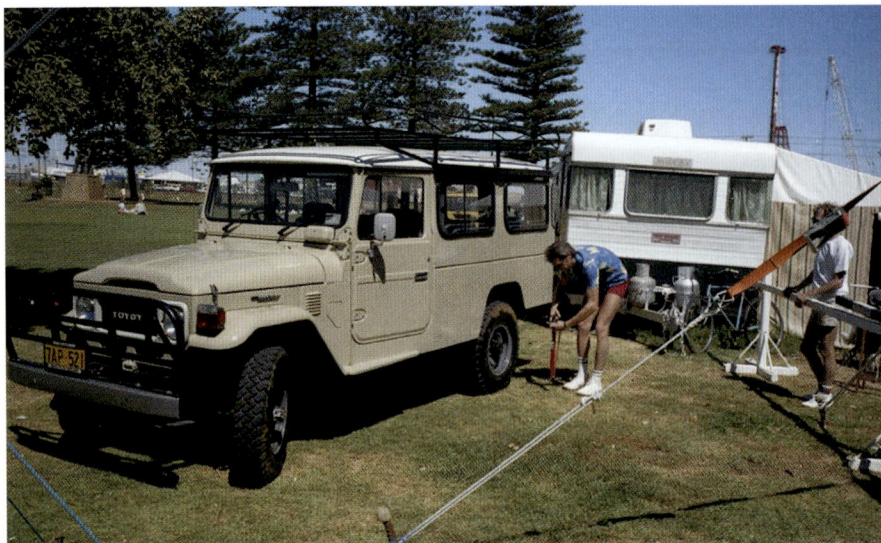

Rod and Charmian get a brand new Toyota Land Cruiser, Fremantle

Fremantle was lovely, and everyone worked hard and had a great time. It was just before the America's Cup yacht race that brought Fremantle to the world's attention, so we unknowingly enjoyed what would be its last days as a sleepy fishing harbour before it all changed. I started each day at Papa Luigi's restaurant with coffee and sometimes an ice cream. They gave me a Papa Luigi's tee shirt that I wore out during the tour of Australia because it was washed so many times. Never before or since did I receive so many comments about an item of clothing, or requests to have me give it away: 'I know that place. Oh, the ice cream!'

The company truck wasn't ready, so I drove a hire truck up to Geraldton for our first gig outside the Perth area, and got a taste of the open road for the first time. I had the company of John Etheridge, the guitarist, who was also doing a gig in Geraldton, for the whole journey. Once we had seen the last of the Perth suburbs, we met no other vehicle all day. *All day!* Had it not been for the signs informing us that Geraldton was ahead of us, I'd have said we were on the wrong road. It was clearly going to be a new experience.

As far as we knew, no other theatre company had attempted to do a tour of Australia like this. To their credit, David Blenkinsop's team at the university-based company of the Festival of Perth dug deep into twenty years of savings to fund it. It soon became clear that those pockets were going to have to be very deep, in fact all the way down to the shoestrings.

Following a day off in the sand dunes by the sea, where the new Nissan Patrols and Toyota Land Cruisers got severely tested, we went back south to perform shows at every town from Bunbury to Esperance. This is one of the few parts of the vast state of Western Australia which are green on the satellite view. It is a stunningly beautiful coastline with amazing beaches and the tallest trees in Australia, a species of eucalyptus called karri. I stopped at a place called Pemberton with Joe and Bruno to see the Gloucester Tree, a fifty-eight metre high karri with a tiny weather station and fire lookout at the top. At the time it was the world's tallest climbable

The author's best friend, a Suzuki 185

The tent and vehicles for the tour of Australia, Geraldton

lookout tree. Set in a spiral all the way up are 153 pegs for climbing, so you could go all the way up the fifty-eight metres. You would need to be fairly fit to do it, which we were, but that's not the hard bit. Impressed with the views from the metal cage lookout, you are less impressed with the way the tree starts to sway with any breath of wind. But there is only one thing left to do (no, not peeing off it!) and that's to go back down the same way you came up.

This is when it gets scary, because you have to look down to find, with your trailing foot, the next peg below the one your other foot is resting on. Are you with me? You could *feel* for it, but it takes too long, and besides you want to see what your foot is putting its weight on. It's weird, but this isn't a problem going up. I suppose it's a bit like the confidence you have driving fast going forward that you wouldn't have going that fast in reverse.

So, what with all the swaying going on, suddenly it dawns on you that it's not fun any more – it's just a flimsy spindle, and you're *ten times* higher than a two-storey house! It was exhilarating, but I was glad to get back to terra firma, even if this strange Australian terra was upside-down.

Bruno taking a giant leap for mankind as we geared up for a tour
that had never been attempted by a theatre company before.

That's another thing – did you know that the moon is also upside-down there? And that if you want to survive, you have to get used to south being 'cold' and north being 'hot', and that the sun travels across the northern sky as it does its daily thing going east to west. In the Aussie desert the stars twinkle visibly at five degrees above the horizon, so it's like being in an IMAX cinema. I soon learned to find the Southern Cross in this vast canopy, get my bearings, and carry on.

By this time, I had got the proper truck for the tour. It was eleven and a half metres long, a Leader with a Caterpillar engine and eight forward gears. The gear stick had a pneumatic collar that you flipped up to go from the first set of four to the upper set of four. I met a stocky Australian chap who demonstrated how to drive it going around an athletics track in Perth. When it was my turn to try it, I said, 'There's something wrong with the clutch, it won't depress.'

He climbed back in, shoving me into the passenger seat. After a couple of successful goes, he said, 'There's something wrong with your fucking leg, mate!' I felt pathetic. I felt like if this bristling Aussie farted in my general direction, I'd be blown out of the cab.

Taro (asleep), Pureza, Paul, Ted, Simon and John Etheridge in Geraldton

At the end of the tour the following year, I had a brute of a left leg built of solid muscle that was always telling the wimpy right one to grow up. If I'd been let off walking in the outback, I would have gone round and round in circles.

ON ALL OUR TOURS WE CONSTANTLY met great people, who loved the kind of theatre we created, invited us to amazing places, and watched adoringly as we ate them out of house and home, drained their wine cellars and danced with their daughters. When we left them to pick up the pieces and disappeared in a cloud of dust, they ached for the loss and the vacuum it left in their lives, because Footsbarn was larger than life. It was larger than the sum of its parts. The exuberant energy, humour and zest for life were infectious and all-consuming.

We were all party to this showbiz illusion, hell-bent on keeping the grand mystique of it alive because it was so addictive. Watching an audience fall in love was a sheer delight. So many people became besotted and wanted to get under the skin of Footsbarn: maybe the magic would rub off on them, and their lives would be the richer for it. It wasn't rock and roll, although we had an affinity with that culture, and it wasn't celebrity and riches, but it was a cult-type following which had its charms and advantages.

Meeting good people in the tiny hamlet of Denmark near Albany in Western Australia reminded me of this, and then the new land of Oz didn't seem so strange anymore. They were generous, wholesome people who just wanted to acknowledge that we had brightened their lives in this remote place because they had never seen anything like it before. They threw parties and showered us with generous gifts and food.

Map of Australia

Spencer with the Nissan Patrols

So on we went, bracing ourselves for the trip across the Nullarbor Plain. We took the only road north out of Esperance and turned right at Norseman. From there it was 1,600 kilometres on the longest straight road in the world, east towards Adelaide. It was about nine days before I got to Adelaide in the truck. But first, a word about Norseman.

Named after a horse that accidentally hoofed up a huge nugget of gold, it became another small town in the goldfields region, like Coolgardie and Kalgoorlie further north. I stayed at a hotel in Norseman reading up on goldfields history from the 1890s. The job of bringing water to these outback towns was left to Irish engineer C.Y. O'Connor, originally from County Meath, who had already achieved success in New Zealand and was now busy with Fremantle Harbour. The poor fella was harassed and vilified in the press and in the Western Australia parliament – both said the projects were doomed to failure – and sadly took his own life in 1894. But his designs for both Fremantle Harbour and the Goldfields Water Supply Scheme were completed successfully by 1904 and are still operational today. Maybe the Aussies' idea of a 'fair go' for everybody wasn't quite so forthright in the gold rush era.

At the bar in the hotel I noticed the nice tile work around the front of the old counter; it even had a tiled gutter that disappeared through a hole where the bar met the wall. Wait a minute, says I. Surely the miners didn't just stand there and relieve themselves of too much beer intake without having to go to the . . . noooo, surely not? Yes, they did! I scurried away, history lesson over, to fill the truck full of diesel and tried to imagine what five and a half tons of gold would actually look like – the amount extracted from this one-horse town since Norseman tripped over that nugget in 1892.

Then, not far down the road, Bruno turned the costume truck on its side. In fairness to Bruno, who was a salt-of-the-earth French technician and a good pal, he hadn't been driving at all for long. We had both been obliged to pass a heavy-goods vehicle test in Perth before we were let loose on Aussie roads. He wasn't hurt, and it wasn't really of any great significance, as the contents of the truck were so light it made it easy to get the truck back on its wheels. No, what was weird was that when the accident happened, Bruno, in shock and rage at himself, forgot all his English and was walking round the fallen truck in circles, cursing away in French, and the first person on the scene to help him was another Frenchman! What were the chances? He was probably the only other Frenchman for five hundred kilometres in any direction. The lengths some people will go to meet a fellow countryman!

A Blast (Furnace) from the Past

Around this time, a nauseating melancholy descended upon me. At first I thought it was some kind of homesickness, but I kept thinking about Whyalla, a coastal town in South Australia where we had done a couple of shows. It was a big industrial port making steel, exporting iron ore and building naval ships at the end of a railway line from Iron Knob, a big inland hill full of iron ore. Something about it had got under my skin, and I couldn't figure what or why. Why Whyalla?

South Australia reminded me so much of England in the 1950s. The cricket clubs with old wooden pavilions reminded me of my father playing in the Cheshire villages when I was a boy. And then it hit me. My father had spent most of his working life at an iron foundry called Wyman's of Warrington. I used to 'help' him sometimes with the company accounts in his office on Saturday mornings, playing with the huge adding machines when I was five or six. Then he'd take me to see the blast furnaces working in the foundry, where the men wore goggles and padded protective clothing against the heat. I loved the way the sparks danced across the foundry floor when they released the molten metal, flowing like burning golden syrup from the furnace.

So that was one connection with Whyalla, but it didn't explain the sense of nostalgia and longing that I found so overwhelming. My birthday happened to coincide with our visit to Whyalla, so on the third of May 1985 I was thirty-five, and it dawned on me that that was the key to it. My father was thirty-five when I was born, and that meant he was already seventy when I was in Australia. This weird set of coincidences had induced a worrying sense of loss, and if I were honest with myself I'd have to admit it was about the loss of my youth. Joseph Campbell, author of *The Hero with a Thousand Faces*, said in an interview with Bill Moyers that so much of human life is coming to terms with loss. Loss of a parent, loss of money, loss of health, loss of vigour, loss of teeth and loss of youth are going to come to most of us.

Don't get me wrong – I wasn't running to seed. I still felt like a fit young man. But it was that number thirty-five, the age when one generation begat another, that triggered the realisation in me that the clock was ticking. And that probably has a lot to do with what I'm doing right now, having reached seventy myself. As Tom Waits says in the movie *Rumble Fish*, 'How much I got? I got thirty-five summers left. Think about it. Thirty-five summers.' Once I knew what it was I felt better and the melancholy went away. I phoned my Dad in Wales. It was my parents' fortieth wedding anniversary, and the whole family were there except me. Then I felt homesick!

South Australia

Adelaide was nice. It has an air of class about it, probably boosted by the claim that it was the only state not settled by convicts. We looked forward to going back there to make a new show. But this time around, we did some shows for the brilliant children's festival called the Come Out Festival. They were real pioneers in the arts-for-children arena. I mean real arts, not just kiddies entertainment. We had a great time but by the end of the stay we felt autumn was approaching and it was time to go north for the winter. (Don't you mean 'fly south' for the winter? No, I've told you once already.)

The road north was notoriously bad from Port Augusta to Alice Springs, so the caravans went by train. My caravan went behind the Leader truck for the first time, after I had a tow hitch fitted at the back. The Nissans, Toyotas, trucks and school bus went up the dirt road known as the Stuart Highway, not to be confused with the Sturt Highway between Sydney and Adelaide. It was 2,834 kilometres from Port Augusta to Darwin via Alice Springs and Tennant Creek. We were warned about the red dust that got into every crack and crevice, so we had to seal all doors and windows.

There was a sign by the roadside just where the tarmacadam ran out. It was meant to inform motorists coming from the other direction that you were entering something more civilised. What *we* saw, flashing by, was what someone had daubed in red paint on the back of the sign, 'Hell Ahead'. All the dirt roads in Australia were affected by weathering, and a particularly annoying feature was the rivulets or ribbed effect running across the roads. Our nickname for

The Leader truck with my motorbike lashed to the bull bars

the road to Alice was Corrugation Street. If you got the vehicle up to sixty miles an hour (around a hundred kilometres an hour), which you could do easily in the Nissans, you virtually skimmed the corrugations and rode out the bumps. The Leader couldn't quite manage that speed in safety, so I enjoyed a thousand-kilometre trip with a bone-shaking ride. Near Woomera, I had my first tyre blowout.

I had already abandoned the idea of towing my caravan behind the truck, since this had proved disastrous – the truck treated it like a rag doll tied to the tail of a tiger. Only a hundred klicks out of Port Augusta, I stopped the truck to see if the caravan was still there because I could never see it in the rear-view mirrors. It was still there, thank God. When I opened the caravan door, things fell out, which wasn't a good sign. The interior looked like it had been ransacked by the FBI. All the cupboard doors were open, and the floor was strewn with smashed plates, broken pots of jam, books and hundreds of photographic slides and negatives. At least the fridge door was locked, but the fridge itself had done a jig around the caravan and looked guilty, caught out of place when the music stopped. The caravan had to be towed behind one of the Nissans, where it was much better behaved.

The Leader after ploughing through the Outback floods,
Coober Pedy, South Australia

I slept overnight close to the garage that fixed the tyre. I'd got to the garage office wheeling the huge offending tyre at 5.30 in the evening. The man behind the counter grinned and said, 'The bad news is: we're closed. The good news is: have a cold beer, mate.' As I drifted off to sleep that evening, I kept wondering why the name Woomera was so familiar to me. It was just a speck on the outback map. In the middle of the night it came to me and I sat up with a start. Get me out of here! This is where they did nuclear bomb testing in the 1950s! Luckily, this was before *The Simpsons*, so I didn't get three-eyed fish for breakfast. But the sickening taste of bore water didn't help with my increasing concern about the quality of life travelling in the outback. Whatever about the water, you could always rely on one thing right across Australia. At any truck stop or gas station, no matter how small, you could get a decent steak sandwich. (In Victoria, where they were more genteel, you might see a roadside sign offering Devons, which usually meant tea and scones with Devonshire cream could be found inside.)

In Coober Pedy, it rained for the first time in years and the red dust turned to red mud. The younger children in the town thought the sky was falling. An unusual place, Coober Pedy. Residents live underground because it's so hot. You could have an opal mine in your own house, with a mineral rock face, rich in opal seams, down the corridor just past the end bedroom. And many people did.

A hundred and twenty kilometres south of Alice Springs, one of the front wheels caught fire and seized the bearings. Bruno was travelling with me at the time. It was his quick reactions in putting the fire out that saved the situation from being worse. Henry fixed the truck after a new axle was flown out from Melbourne. We had to go back and forth from Alice several times, not only to fix the truck but to get stuff out of it for the shows. We needed to be swift, because the abandoned truck was vulnerable in the desert. A note in the cab window saying 'Back in five minutes' wasn't going to fool anyone.

The shows went brilliantly in Alice Springs, and the locals loved them. At the end of the run we had a day off. Paddy invited me to visit Ayers Rock on a day trip with the kids. I was exhausted from all the driving and going to and fro across the desert, and the thought of another long drive was a rock too far. It was a pity to have been so close and not see one of the country's major attractions, but we faced another long-haul drive: Darwin was the next gig, and we were only halfway there. We also had an invitation to Aboriginal communities in the Northern Territory at the behest of the Aboriginal Arts Board. Thankfully it was the dry season. The wet season in Darwin is insufferable, apparently.

Luckily, we got a spot on the local TV station news to promote the shows when we got to Darwin. I don't remember doing TV interviews much for Footies but I do remember this one. An enthusiastic and smartly dressed young man and his cameraman came down to the camp while we were setting up the tent. His huge frame loomed over me as he described in detail all the questions he was going to ask, like how we had got here, what type of theatre shows could the audiences expect, what was it like having a tent as a venue and so on and so forth. All the while I was preparing my answers mentally logging them all in order and trying not to sweat.

Once the newscaster had given him the nod from back at the station and we were rolling, he announced to the viewers: 'We are talking to Tid Turton from Foots baarn Theatre down at the paark in town.' At this point, a look of panic came over him and an awkward silence hovered in the air until the cameraman coughed behind him.

'What's it all about, Tid?' he blurted out, thrusting a shaking microphone in my face.

Fortunately, all the answers I'd lined up in my brain came trotting out like I was a seasoned journo, and all my nervous beads of sweat seemed to have magically transferred to *his* dripping face. After the interview he bought me a beer and we chatted away about football which seemed to be safer ground for him, poor fella. Anyway, the tent was full a couple of days later so I must have got the story across to the Darwin public somehow.

The Top End and Its Aboriginal Communities

At the Top End, as the Aussies called it, where the vast reaches of the Northern Territory meet the north coast, slightly different rules applied, it seemed. We were aware of the greater numbers of Aboriginal people around, especially in Katherine, halfway between Alice and Darwin where the Katherine Gorge had become a big tourist attraction. It was crocodile country now that we were above the Tropic of Capricorn. 'Freshies' you could swim with if you dared; 'salties' were a lot bigger, and under no circumstances would you enter the water with any of them around.

Australians have shortened nicknames for everything, as well as other slang terms. 'Chuck a few snaggers on the barbie, Bruce, a few rellies are coming over.' Snaggers are sausages – you can guess the rest of it. A sign by the roadside with 'O nite vans' printed on it meant there was a rentable caravan available for travellers who

Everyone gathered in Darwin for a photo before Petal left for school in the UK.
Back row, left to right: Paul, Margaret, Paddy, Simon, Pureza, Suze, Angela.
Next row: Rod, Freddy, Maggie, Carlie, Dave J, Spencer, Henry.
Next row: Charmian, Josie, Bibo holding Zana, Petal, Joe, Gio, Marta.
Front row: Julie holding Kes, Nico, Rowan and Bunty (Freddy's mum).
John, Ted and Dave H not in photo.

were falling asleep driving a car. If you had a 'Ute' you were lucky enough to have a pick-up truck or utility vehicle to swan around in and there were a lot of them in Australia.

A lot of the things you hear about Australian wildlife are true, like frogs living under the rim of the toilet, seven-foot-long black snakes, king brown snakes, funnel web spiders and nasty jellyfish. We saw them all. The pain from a box jellyfish sting is so bad that swimmers regularly carry bottles of vinegar or urine, either of which helps to relieve the pain. Bill Bryson's brilliant book about Australia has a sobering account of a brush with a box jellyfish that describes just how bad the pain can be. I managed to avoid the deadly type of stings and bites, but the encounter with frogs is unnerving because you don't know they are there until you get off the loo and flush. It's the gush of water that dislodges them from under the rim.

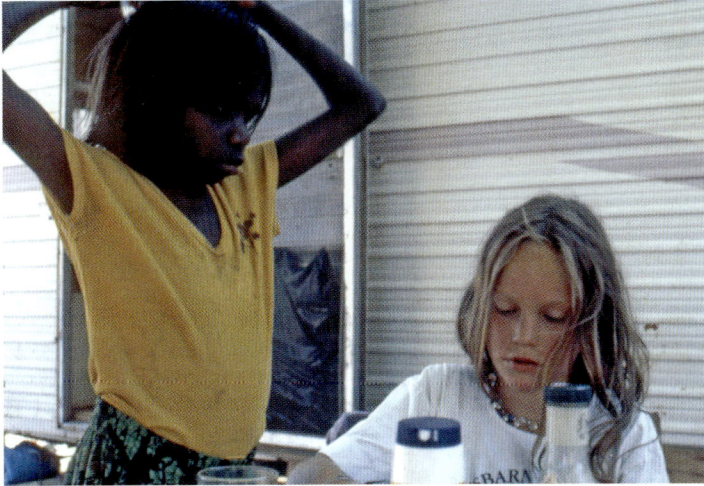

Jose with one of the Aborigine girls, Oenpelli

White Australians were not normally allowed in the Aboriginal community territories, which covered thousands of square miles, but some white medics and staff were there at the village settlements to help if necessary. So we felt privileged to visit three different communities in the Northern Territory, perform shows there and work with them on outdoor events.

My first day in Gunbalanya (historically called Oenpelli when we were there), I remember feeling like I was an alien on my own planet. For a start, there was a lot of wailing and keening going on, and when I asked a nurse what the commotion was about, she explained that a young couple had eloped against the wishes of the elders. When the couple had a baby, the elders 'pointed the bone' at them and the baby died. The nurse said she had seen the baby a

Maggie in Oenpelli with one of the nurses

Daisy, Petal and Carlie in Darwin

couple of days previously and there was nothing wrong with it; she couldn't explain the baby's demise.

Wondering whether to believe this or not, I got on with setting up for the shows. I took some photographs but it wasn't easy, because the native people's shyness overcame their curiosity. I walked to a house raised up off the ground on small stilts; it was in lovely condition. When no one answered my calls or knocks, I peered inside the door. There wasn't a stick of furniture in its two rooms, nor anyone at home. On the bare floorboards a television sat, merrily broadcasting some Aussie soap to a family that had probably gone off on a walkabout several months earlier.

When we got the tent up and running, ready for the *Circus Tosov* show, no one turned up to see it. We had been advised to charge an entrance fee, which we set at a very low $2. The sun had gone down and it was a fine moonless night, so now we were told to knock off the lights – all of them, and the house music too. After ten minutes the locals started to edge forward out of the darkness. I could just make

Petal, Marta and Margaret, Darwin

out eyes and teeth coming towards me as we brought the lights up a little to help them make their way through to the tent arena. Each person dropped a small ball of paper into my hand as they passed me, and for the first half-hour of the show I was flattening out the $2 notes that, for some reason, they'd screwed into a ball. I never found out why. It was just another thing you didn't bother to question.

Inside the tent it was pandemonium as the audience excitement couldn't be contained. Several times, the show had to be stopped as over-eager women who wanted to join in the show and clamber on stage were cajoled back to their seats by Rod in his Rockin' Ronnie Conker role. There were opportunities for audience participation in this show, but only when the actors were in control, not the other way round. At the end of a chaotic show, Paddy was ushering people out, his face still smothered with white make-up and sweat. A large Aboriginal woman was beaming at him, so he asked her if she'd enjoyed the show. 'Oh, yes,' she said. 'Me laughing. Me laughing, crying, farting.'

An all-Aborigine audience at the clown show

We did some workshops with the indigenous adults while our own children shared lessons and painting with their children. The evenings were a bit weird because the pub was inside a huge cage, and it was closed until six o'clock. It was well known that Aboriginal people had a problem with drink: many indigenous peoples lack enzymes that allow the body to break down the alcohol, resulting in a super-fast conversion to sugars without the body being able to take it out of the bloodstream. Consequently, they tended to get drunk faster than we would. Plus there were genetic mutations that pass on the addictive nature once alcoholism is established, which is why a lockout was self-imposed on the village pub. Footsbarn, too, it should be said, had a collective fondness for alcohol, so things could get lively in the evenings. The winter sun drops like a stone in the tropics, and darkness falls quickly. The lights came on, the cage was opened and everyone got pissed on Victoria bitter.

I asked a young man who had distinctly paler skin if he was . . . I was struggling to find the right words after 'Are you err . . .', and nothing came out. Eventually he helped me out.

'D'yer mean a yella fella? Oh, yes, I'm one of them, all right.' He smiled and raised his tinny. I told him that my mother's maiden name was from Sweden, so I suppose that made me a yella fella as well, and we got on just fine.

THE YOUNGER GUYS SHOWED US WHERE WE could swim and came along for the craic to these beautiful lakes in the forest surrounded by rock cliffs and deep, clear, cooling water. It was absolute bliss.

'Why aren't you coming in?' we shouted, splashing about in the middle of the lake.

'Ah, no,' they said seriously, 'there's a spirit in there.' Seeing the look of horror and panic on our faces, they burst their sides laughing. 'It's okay, it won't affect you lot.'

Given a holiday for a couple of weeks, some of us headed for Kakadu National Park, where it was so beautiful that the morning catchphrase became, 'Oh no, not another day in paradise!'

During my time with the group, there were break-ups, couples falling out and then falling in with someone else. Some adults clashed horribly, and yet we all got on with the job and looked out for each other. It was normal enough for guys in their thirties, and it's not something I'm even tempted to write about because it just becomes soap opera stuff. Some decided to quit and move on for a whole variety of reasons. Some actors left only to rejoin a couple of years later.

Paintings at the school, Oenpelli

Simon was at such a crossroads when we were in Darwin. He would often ask me if there was life after Footsbarn. He would joke about what the Progue Master had in store for him, as he put it (probably referring to the great god that programmes one's life). Perhaps the lack of fulfilment as a theatre percussionist was now weighing more heavily on his mind, and a desire to be a full-time musician was bubbling away under the surface. With his relationship crumbling I was eager to help him and the upcoming holiday offered us an opportunity to get away from it all. I heard that Bali was a paradise island, only a short flight across the sea to Indonesia, that had recently opened up tourism to an Australian market.

'Yes, there is a flight from Darwin to Denpasar each week,' the travel agent downtown told me. 'Sorry, it's full, but we'll put you on the waiting list.'

Two days before the holiday began, the agent called to say one person could go. I suggested that Simon go alone, and I would try for the following week's flight. I went with him to the airport, packed with a bag and passport just in case. As I was wishing Simon the best of luck, a woman approached from the check-in desk.

'Can I see your passport, Mr Turton? That's fine. A woman has just turned up here with an out-of-date passport, and we know the Indonesian authorities won't let her in. So, you lucky thing, you're on your way to Bali. Have a nice trip.'

Bali, Indonesia

The contrast between Bali and the vast expanses of Australia is so stark it could be another world. Around every corner and in every nook and cranny, Bali offers endless gems of interest and visual delights, along with scents and sounds that send your mind spinning with previously uncharted experiences and stimuli. Our bicycles took us all over the island, from the south coast to a volcanic mountain, to the north coast and eventually to Kuta. This was a 'white Australian black hole' that we'd been advised to avoid, but it turned out to be better than we imagined.

The first day in Ubud, the inland village and cultural centre, immersed us deeply in Balinese rituals with dance and music. We eagerly accepted our baptism into the strange mix of Hindu and Buddhist culture. In those days the Monkey Forest road leading away from the village centre still passed by a football pitch and rice fields. Both the pitch and fields are gone and it's all built up. Bali had barely started gearing up for tourists, but here in Ubud there were already slightly annoying guys touting for business with shouts across the street: 'Hello, transport.' Their overdeveloped patter had already lost any sense of a question to it. It was more like a barked statement that informed you, 'Hello, we're going to take you somewhere whether you like it or not, and it's going to cost you.'

My cheery, confident reply, 'Hello, transport yourself' usually made them laugh and go harangue someone else. In reality, the Balinese people were so likeable and friendly, you couldn't get too annoyed.

Simon and I seemed to be doing okay getting round the island with English. The curious phrase, 'Hello, where do you come prom?' sprang from every child's lips as soon as they saw us passing on our bikes. I heard it said about three hundred times in two weeks. The children, unlike the adults, were keen to be photographed. It was fine the first day, but it became such a clamour that I had to just pretend to click the shutter after that.

I remember being gobsmacked by the way everything was so colourfully decorated. Every little bamboo way station, built in the fields to commemorate some religious ceremony, was left to softly decay with red ribbons flying and bright-yellow decorative cloth intact. Every stone effigy of the elephant-headed Ganesh or the monkey god Hanuman was adorned with fresh hibiscus flowers behind the ears and chequered cloth for a skirt. Offerings of rice were put

Ubud, Bali

out mornings and afternoons on little plaited trays, and even though the local mangy dog would come and devour it, the people seemed to accept that it was all part of the natural cycle.

Gamelan music wafted down streets and across the fields. Every day turned up a new experience. Black rice pudding for breakfast. Yellow waxy fingers of succulent jackfruit in the market (I'd never heard of it). The sultry beauty of the Balinese people and their welcoming nature was kindness itself. I was intoxicated by it all, and we both went without alcohol for two weeks quite happily until the last night in Kuta.

When we ran out of road heading for the mountains, we got off the bikes and pushed them across the rocks and boulders, not realising that it was going to be a long push at this stage. Had it not been for a truck bouncing slowly up the road that stopped for us to jump aboard, we'd still be pushing. The next place was Penelokan, nearly 1,500 metres above sea level by Lake Batur in the shadow of the volcano of the same name. Thanking the truck driver when he dropped us at Penelokan, we got our bikes down and rode round the lake with a view to tackling the volcano on foot the following morning. When we got to the small village at the base of the volcano, we noticed that the villagers were in some consternation.

Balinese society is very strict, and decorum had to be observed even among tourists. Wearing appropriate clothes and scarves when entering the temples was mandatory. But this seemed to be more serious. Here, a young man from Brisbane, whose wealthy Pakistani father had sent him off on a world tour, had made his first stop in Bali and had fallen at the first fence. This delightful youngster, probably a dozen years younger than us, looking every inch a potential film star, was passionately in love with the local beauty. The teenage girl felt exactly the same, but here he was, distraught and asking me for advice. Me? Advice? I would think about it overnight. Seeing them together that evening, my heart went out to them. Her in the traditional colourful costume with a flower in her hair. Him with

Rice growing on terraces and drying in bunches, Bali

his immaculate white shirt and jeans. Two worlds clashing and, as always, love and desire rising above it all. They were obviously smitten with each other. And here they were snatching a precious hour together before the elders, ever watchful, restricted their, erm, movements.

Over breakfast in the morning I suggested he take his father's gift and go experience the world out there. He could always write to his lover. I tried to sound earnest rather than flippant with consoling words, but in truth I had no idea what was best for him. I wished him luck, knowing that either way, go or stay, it was going to be a real test for him, and maybe a painful ecstasy.

Simon and I left the breakfast table, nearly knocking over a small boy who was trying to sell bottles of cold Coca-Cola from a big round basket. 'How much? What? Too much. Sorry, little fella' and we rushed away to scramble up the volcano. He seemed crestfallen, as there weren't many tourists about. After two hours climbing the mountain, sometimes on our hands and knees, we were staring into the steaming volcano from the rim. The rock was hot to the touch, it was midday and we were gasping. As if on cue, there was the same small boy with his enormous basket of Coke, only now it was twice the price. 'Okay, go on, then.' Coke had never been so enjoyable.

Because we were so high, still over a thousand metres above sea level at the start of our next part of the journey, it was a downhill bike ride all the way to Lovina on the north coast. After half an hour or so, with the sea still beyond our vision through the haze, I stopped to discard a layer of clothing as we were dropping out of the cool mountain climate. Outside a little country house, yet another beautiful young woman was washing clothes and minding a toddler in the garden.

As I stood astride the bike, I rolled up a cigarette, while the woman must have said to the little boy something like, 'Go look on the road. There's a spaceman out there on a bicycle.' He ran out from the garden, looking the wrong way, and stood there in the deserted road, marvelling at the distant haze. The sound of my lighter clicking behind him made him turn round, and then he nearly jumped out of his shoes, staggering backwards and disappearing into the hedge. I looked at his mother and we started laughing. Why I should remember this, such a seemingly insignificant moment from the flotsam and jetsam of my life, I've no idea. Maybe I wanted to remember everything on that wonder-packed adventure.

Heat gathered around us on the way down, as if we were descending into some kind of giant kitchen, along with all the sounds of busy traffic and smells of cooking food. After a few days lazing and swimming in the sea at Lovina, we returned to Ubud the long way, around the mountains to avoid any taxing climbs. South of Ubud village I discovered the mask-maker Oka and his brother and family. We became instant friends and he showed me all the techniques of his woodworking craft and his painting skills. His work was so exquisite it had made him famous by the time I visited him again, years later in the 1990s. It was then he told me about his international exhibition, saying, 'Me, little Oka. I had never been outside my own village, and they sent me to Tokyo! It was a terrible shock.'

Simon learned to play the Gamelan with Ida Bagus and then we watched the shadow puppets at the local theatre. Everything looked hand-crafted. We wanted to buy everything we saw and couldn't, of course, except I must have spent a fortune on film. From the landscapes and rice terraces to the temple architecture, craftwork and textiles, not to mention the people and their costumes, it was all so captivating, and my trusty Leica M2 camera was working overtime.

We met an elderly German guy when we got back to Ubud to return the bikes. He said he'd been here before the war, in 1935, and wanted to see what it was like fifty years later. He described a real paradise island unknown to tourism. The women, young and old, were all bare-chested. Now, the only women who were topless were the very old and those represented in the Balinese paintings and tapestries.

Sharing a hut in Kuta with two young Aussie surfers, who seemed to exist on peanut butter and honey sandwiches, we knew our trip to Paradise Island was nearly over. I turned on a radio for the first time in two weeks. News interrupted the music: 'The Greenpeace ship, the *Rainbow Warrior*, has been sunk in Auckland.' Wakey, wakey, Ted. The real world awaits you.

SIMON DECIDED TO LEAVE THE COMPANY when we got back to Darwin, and made plans to see his brother in Brazil. And there he settled in Rio for thirty years. He left behind his beloved cymbals and gongs that he and I had chosen together at the UFIP factory in Pistoia in Italy. They were essential for the *King Lear* show. No storm without them. Steve took over the percussion with some of the other actors. Gunga was called in from Amsterdam when it was time to create the new show in Adelaide. Originally from Glasgow, he was an admirable replacement musician for Simon, and he brought with him an unmistakable Scottish accent and sense of humour, along with his partner, Muneca from Surinam.

So I lost one friend in Darwin that July. By the end of August I'd found another. She was a photographer, and that was just what I was looking for, someone to collaborate with me for an exhibition about the whole tour to be shown at the Adelaide Festival the following March. On our first evening out together in Brisbane, she drove the wrong way down a one-way street and got a right telling off and a ticket from the traffic cop. Wanting to impress me, she was understandably mortified. In the long run, she must have done something right, because we were married three years later.

Queensland

Reluctantly leaving Kakadu National Park and the Northern Territory, we faced another punishing long drive across Queensland before reaching the coast at Townsville. Some of those drives across the outback severely tested the will to live. It isn't made any easier by the endless sameness of the landscape and vegetation, and always the unforgiving ribbon of road that disappeared at the horizon where a distant blue ridge mountain never seemed to get any closer. Being so used to landscapes fashioned by human hand over centuries in Europe, my eyes were accustomed to look for patterns, hedgerows, field furniture and farm machinery, church steeples, anything of architectural interest and any geological feature that pleased the eye. The stark nature of the outback, with its thousands of kilometres of red soil, dotted here and there with gum trees, made it unreadable. As a result, the places on the way round Australia that featured unusual rock formations, like the Pinnacles and the Devil's Marbles, were mandatory stops and, in truth, they were extraordinary.

In the cab of the truck I had the company of Sade and her *Diamond Life* album, which I played countless times that year. Whenever I hear 'Smooth Operator' now, I'm sent back in time to the land of Oz. There were a few things I remember, besides kangaroos, that we would never have experienced in Europe. One was the occasional sight of a flock of parrots or lorikeets suddenly crossing our path with a flash of brilliant colours. Another was getting out of the way of road trains because they tended not to stop for anything. Consequently, sightings of dead cattle were a common occurrence, and we had to take evasive action closing the windows as fast as we could because the smell, when the animal was in the bloated phase, was sickening. You could see them from a distance looking like giant balloons with legs sticking out. The last phase was just a collapsed carcass of leather-covered bones after nature and an army of various insects had done their worst. That was okay – by that stage the smell had gone.

*John, Paddy, Dave H, and Bruno in Brisbane with the Banyan
tree that made an appearance as the background to the Macbeth poster*

Paddy (in the mask) and Rod at the Warana Festival parade, Brisbane

Fortunately, the Leader truck was robust enough not to be bothered by too much, with its huge bull bars on the front. The only creature I ran over was a long black snake, but I did have an argument with a mini twister, or dust devil as the Aussies called them. I could see it coming across the barren landscape about a kilometre away to my left and heading in the same direction that I was. It wasn't like the ones you see in America, where the dense clouds form a funnel and touch the ground, taking Dorothy and Toto and everything with it. This was a whorl of dust on a hot sunny day, and our paths converged. It only took a few seconds for the twister to pass through, and I experienced a brief 'brown out' accompanied by a great rushing sound. When the windscreen cleared, I realised I was careering down the opposite carriageway, while the twister meandered off to the right, looking for something else to wreak havoc with. I swore that it picked the truck up off its wheels and put it back down again, but this story only ever elicited a skeptical sneer and I knew nobody believed me.

Shade from trees at any of the RV stops in the desert areas was at a premium. Sometimes a seasoned traveller would be parked under the only available tree long before sundown. Taking advantage of the shade came with a penalty in the form of cacophonous noises from hundreds of parrots, especially grey and pink galahs, that roosted in the tree and argued with each other incessantly. I saw one such camper-van guy who had come up with a solution: he stationed a cannon next to his vehicle that went off automatically every twenty minutes. The enormous bang would send the parrots flying off in a huge cloud high into the sky. By the time they settled back into the tree and slowly built up their unbearable racket, the cannon went off again. Trying to doze off amid this endless round of events, I was left pondering: 'Cannon or parrots, cannon or parrots? Cannon, I suppose. Silly galahs!' (You haven't really experienced Australians unless you've been affectionately ridiculed and called a silly galah.)

Bruno and I had to make a stop at the lovely sounding isolated hamlet of Julia Creek. The best thing about this nondescript place was that it had a breakers yard, full of rusting vehicles of all description. I needed a replacement leaf spring for my caravan and luckily we found an identical caravan on the edge of the vast yard. That was the easy bit. Getting the old leaf spring removed from the found caravan with manual spanners proved to be an ordeal that took three times as long as it should have done. The problem was that after a couple of twists of the spanner while holding on to the axle with the other hand, my face was a seething mass of black flies, seemingly attracted by the sweat dripping from our faces in the intense afternoon heat. Impossible to see anything at this point, the only thing to do was get out from under the caravan and run away, flailing hands and arms like a windmill while Bruno took over for a further twenty seconds, in a continuous round of absurdly comical activity until the spring eventually dropped to the ground. *Run away! Run for it! For God's sake, let's get out of here. Don't forget the spring!*

Mount Isa was the last of the desert stops. A brutal, rust-coloured industrial complex sitting in the middle of an arid area of north-west Queensland, it is the largest copper-smelting and combined producer of lead, silver, copper and zinc in the world. We escaped to the artificial lakes outside the city, where we had picnics in the lovely clear air – which was actually heavy with lead and said to be the most polluted in Australia, made so by the smoke that pours from giant stacks.

It was here that Henry killed a goanna by accident, so he and Taro brought the headless creature back to camp. The goanna is a giant lizard, so we weren't sure if it would be tasty or edible at all if we cooked it. Rod says he was told how to do it by one of the Aboriginal guys. You have to dig a deep pit in the ground, fill it with dry sticks and get a fire going in it. Laying the whole goanna on top, you cover it completely with stones and wait for an hour. When it's done, you throw away the goanna and eat the stones.

Ups and Downs along the Pacific Coast

Reaching Townsville gave us our first sight of the Pacific Ocean and the gorgeous phenomenon of the Pacific sunset, which fills the sky with peachy colours. Even long after the sun has gone down, an afterglow begins and the rays fan out in spectacular streams of red and purple, and any stray wisp of cloud turns electric pink. It's quite unlike anything across the Atlantic.

From this point we would be heading south along the east coast, performing in several towns on a schedule that had us competing with a highly successful Aussie touring version of *The Rocky Horror Show*. At times our schedule overlapped with theirs, and when it did, they usually won in a scrap for an audience.

'Life's a Beach', painting by the author of the magnificent beach at Byron Bay, New South Wales

Two crazy accidents happened one after the other, the first in Townsville and the second in Rockhampton, right on the Tropic of Capricorn. Erecting the tent entailed having the two king poles up and ready to take the enormous weight of the roof canopy. It was raised with winding gear fixed to the bottom of each king pole. A handle would be wound, round and round, sending the canopy up the poles on steel cables. It was slow work and it took effort, but a ratchet on the gear wheel allowed you to rest halfway if you wanted, without the whole thing falling back down. The winding handle was at right angles to the wheel, so you could get two hands on it and push in an arc away from you.

Both winders had to be done at the same time. Spencer was on one, Dave H on the other. Loads of us were on hand for the next stage – putting up the tent walls – so we stood and watched as the huge canopy went higher and higher. For some reason, Spencer's winding handle slipped out of his grip and failed to catch on the ratchet cog. The handle flew back round at about seventy miles an hour and hit him smack in the face, just below the nose. His two front teeth shot out like bullets from a gun, leaving him on the ground, dazed and shocked with blood pouring down his chin.

While someone ran to get first aid, I said, 'Okay, the first thing we do is find the teeth and somebody get some ice.' Everyone looked at me as if I'd lost my mind. 'Come on,' I said, with some urgency. 'If they're not broken, they'll go straight back in.' After a short search scrambling about in the grass, we found them, still in perfect shape. Spencer was packed off to the emergency dentist and returned a while later with his front teeth back in the right place. (Actually, sending him off with the teeth in a bag of ice was okay, but putting them under his tongue for the journey would have been even better.)

Years later Angela told me that wasn't the whole story. She recounted how Spencer had been given two kangaroo teeth as a present from an Aboriginal guy they had befriended before leaving the Top End. Spencer had forgotten them and left them behind, which might have been seen as something of an insult. Who knows? But it's weird.

At the next stop, Rockhampton, we were performing in the splendid municipal theatre, so this time the naughty tent stayed in the truck. The first I knew of this new incident was Paul's muffled cry for help coming from inside the theatre building. Somehow he had been left on stage practising his violin when the lights went out. Trying to find his way in the dark, he fell off the edge of the stage into the orchestra pit, which might not have been such a calamity had he not reached out with his free right hand to save himself. A lamp stand with a protective mesh grille over the light fitting caught his fingers, ripping one of them off in the fall. Fortunate, in as much as it was his bowing hand; he was lucky to escape with the violin and his fret hand intact, along with his teeth and other bits. But it was unfortunate that the digit did not take to being sewn back on when the operation to save it failed. He was back playing soon afterwards with his thumb and three fingers.

Everyone had a great time in Brisbane. It was a refreshing change to be back in a big-city atmosphere. It even had a Chinatown district. We were parked right next to the modern municipal building, which housed everything to do with the Queensland Performing Arts Trust. Not even a deluge that flooded the tent one afternoon could dampen our spirits. We had a great time joining other street entertainers and groups from Papua New Guinea at the Warana Festival parade.

Marta celebrated her twenty-first in Brisbane: a good excuse for another party. She was only seventeen when we'd met in Lisbon, and she'd joined the company when she and Dave H fell in love. Now she was a young mother to two-year-old Giovanni. The other babies in the group were Zana, Kes and Tiam. When Zana was ready to enter the world's stage, she came earlier than expected. This happened to be in a field in Geneva, thwarting all plans for a birth at the next gig the following week. Waddling out of her bus that bright Geneva morning, Charmian had said to me, 'I think I'm going to have this baby today.' Sure enough, that night Rod, the frantic father-to-be, found himself running across the field in the dark to call for an ambulance from the nearest phone box.

Charmian and Zana

When he got back to say it was on the way, Freddy had already come to Charmian's aid and delivered the baby. Angie and Spencer turned up with a book about birthing, so they were able to deal with cutting the cord before the ambulance came. Both mother and baby were fine. Still only six months old by the time we were touring in Australia, Zana repaid her parents for being born on the road by demonstrating that she would only go to sleep in the evenings if she was driven round and round the camp in the Land Cruiser.

Everyone doted on them, especially on Gio, as he was at such a lovely age then. By the time we reached

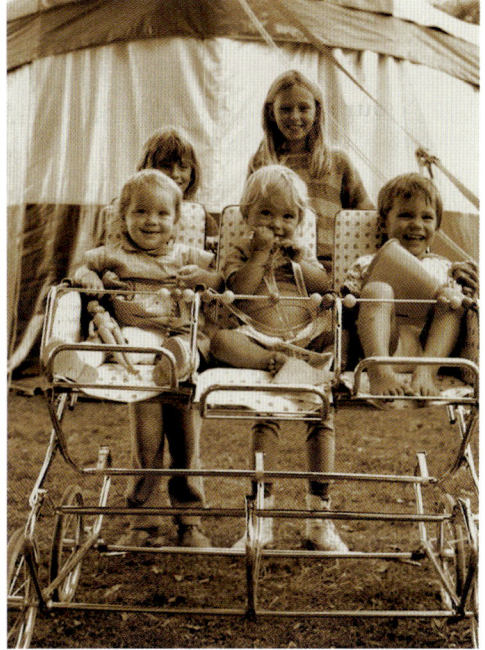

Nico and Carlie with babies Zana, Kes and Gio in Philip Park, Sydney

Adelaide second time round, he was quite independent, wandering around talking to anyone and everyone in English or Portuguese.

There was a loo in the costume workshop on site that I sometimes used in the early mornings before work started, though it was a bit exposed. No door on it for example. One time I was sitting there on the toilet, waiting for something to happen, reading a magazine, when Gio walked in and stood next to me. 'Hello, Gio,' I said. He quickly lost interest in the magazine and plunged his hand between my legs and pulled out whatever he could find. Keeping a tight grip, he looked me in the face and asked, 'Is this your willy?' Before I could answer, he said, 'Let's put it away' and yanked it back down where he found it. Wincing with pain, I just managed to croak, 'Okay.' And then he was off trying on costumes.

Christmas in Melbourne, New Year in Sydney

Christmas in Melbourne was a bit strange, especially eating Christmas pudding in the middle of summer. But I liked the city on the whole, in particular the Italian restaurants down Lygon Street. It's the thinking person's city as well as a gastronomic delight. This week of shows was quickly followed by a trip to Sydney and a set-up in Phillip Park in the centre of the city for new year at the Sydney Festival. This was another long drive but nowhere near as punishing as the dessert drives. The pioneers who built the Hume highway are honoured half way to Sydney at Gundagai with a monument to 'the dog that sat on the tucker box' the strange tale, poem and song with varying degrees of vulgarity that either saved or ruined a drover's lunch, depending on whether you sing the word

Trucks at the base camp, McLaren Vale, South Australia

'sat' or the alternative 'shat'. Anyway, the fabled pooch is in bronze and he admirably collects money via a fountain for the local hospital.

Sydney and its festival were a sheer delight. How can you not like Sydney with its spectacular harbour and gorgeous leafy waterside suburbs stretching all around it? We were blessed with fine weather, good audiences and welcome rave reviews in the papers. But now our attention was shifting towards the joys and excitement of making a new show, so the visits to New South Wales and Victoria seemed to come to an end all too quickly and before 1986 got into its stride we were heading off to South Australia for the second time.

Macbeth, Something Wicked

Here we looked forward to setting up for the next creation, *Macbeth*. It would take about six weeks. We were given a park site beside the McLaren Vale oval sports field. It was in a beautiful broad and shallow valley full of vineyards bordered by the long line of soft-ly rounded Willunga Hills, also known locally as *The Titty Bums*. This region of South Australia south of Adelaide was famous for its lovely wines, so we settled in, befriended the couple who ran the nearby Salopian Inn, and also the owner of the local vineyard (vital-ly important) and tennis court, and went to work.

Macbeth was created for the 1986 Adelaide Festival. It had a tribal theme, with Paddy taking the title character for the first time in a Footsbarn Shakespeare production. All the costumes and masks were made by Charmian and Freddy along with an entourage of helpers led by Angela and Muñeca. *Macbeth's* crown was made of feathers and bones lending him a chief-like authority and alongside Rod's Banquo they made a blood-soaked, battle-weary entrance to the play that set the scene and style for the whole production. Maggie, as *Lady Macbeth*, was probably enjoying one of her finest hours, so to speak, as an actress. But all the cast pulled out the stops and helped make

Pureza, Steve and Gunga rehearsing, McLaren Vale

it another highly inventive and entertaining show, so typical of Footsbarn's creative power at this time. Pureza made great use of her continuous breathing technique, showing off her skill with the didgeridoo during the brief interludes between scenes. Gunga, ever the Scotsman, wore blue makeup all over his face. He was only missing the white X that the Scottish football and rugby fans daub across their cheeks and beards. Great musician, mind you: he could get a tune and a rhythm out of anything. Steve created a lot the music and played several instruments.

Freddy's masks for Macbeth show

Given that any performance of *Macbeth* is going to embody violence and cruelty there were, nevertheless, opportunities for Footsbarn's usual humorous antics, especially with the scene following King Duncan's murder when the Porter, played by Dave, took five minutes to get from one side of the stage to the other to answer the door. Berating Macduff and Lennox for making him rush, rush, rush the Porter keeps up what could only be described as a painstaking shuffle while the unseen callers continue banging on the other side of the door. Stopping to mop a weary brow half way across, Dave milked the audience's screams of laughter. Later in the play when Banquo's ghost appeared, Rod lightened the mood of a normally scary scene by having

Freddy modelling the head gear she made for MacDuff (Photo: Marie Allen)

Banquo cheekily reveal his long line of progeny in the form of finger puppets, one by one with a miniature head painted in his likeness on each of his ten digits. It was a nice touch.

Looking at the bigger picture, the object was to get *Macbeth* to appeal to all kinds of audiences: young and old, in the city or in the country, in theatres or in the tent. If these Footsbarn characters looked the part in their tribal attire and setting, then anyone seeing the play would be likely to identify with them and the base motivations that drive Macbeth and his wife to do their worst, namely greed and ambition. We're not talking about 'savages' here, although the behaviour could be said to be pretty savage. I think it was more about creating a setting that was closer to the origins of human nature and how we all carry those genes from our tribal ancestors. If it worked, the Shakespearean language would flourish like a rose on an ancient briar.

Paddy as Macbeth and Maggie as Lady Macbeth
(Photo: Marie Allen)

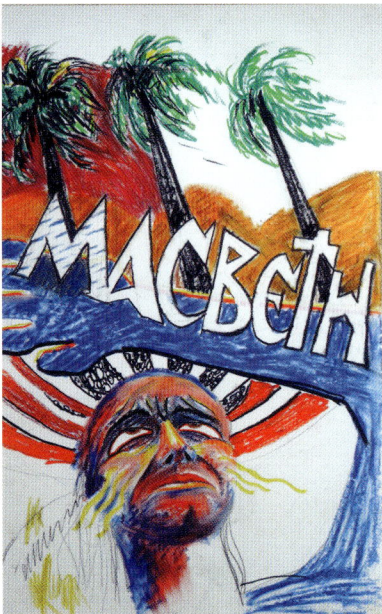

Sketch for Macbeth poster

In the end it did so much more, and the good people from the Adelaide Festival who paid for the production were delighted with the result when the show opened. Paddy had a great time with those wonderful lines, while the witches were suitably haggard wearing strapped-on leathery tits and Balinese-inspired face masks. Maggie was so convincing as Lady Macbeth I imagine she is still trying to wash her blood-stained hands clean. Marie did a brilliant job taking photographs with her Nikon cameras and zoom lenses. My old Leica wasn't up to the job.

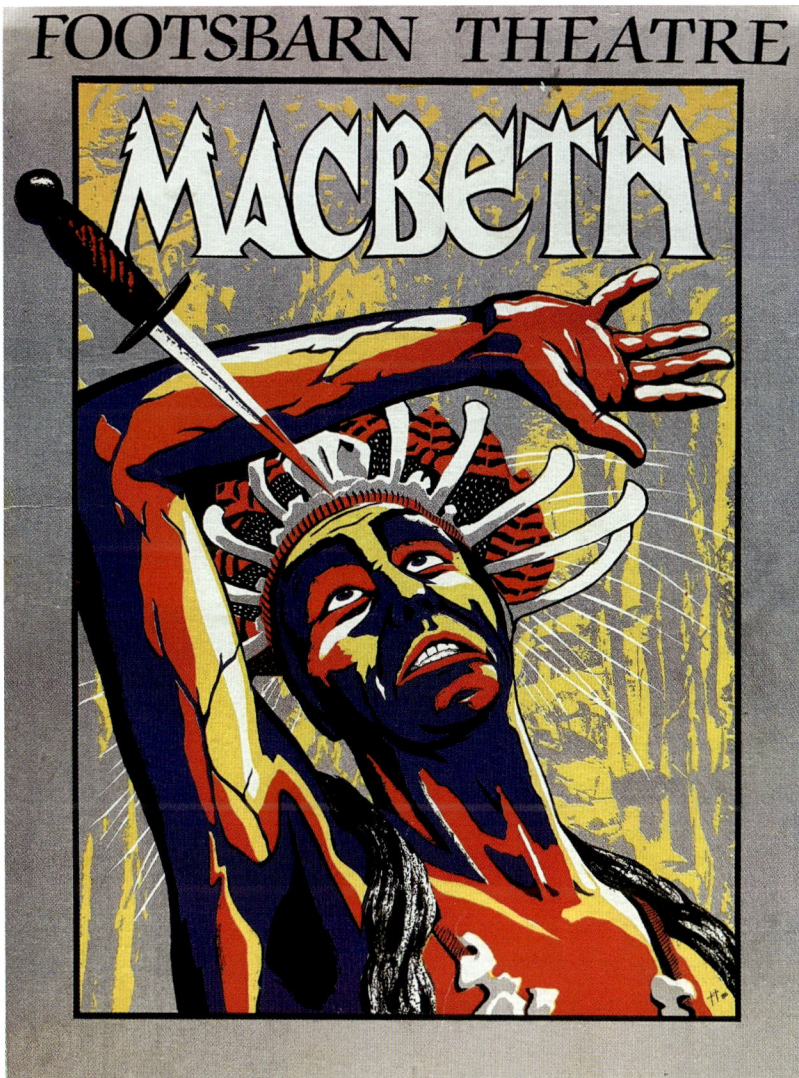

Finished Macbeth poster

Did our meetings with Aboriginal Australians have any influence on the kind of production Footsbarn made of *Macbeth*? Perhaps, but only because we accepted the fact that, as a race or group of tribes, these people had survived and adapted to such a harsh environment for 40,000 years and we acknowledged that that was an awesome achievement. That kind of thing was always going to impress Footies.

Also, we saw more of Australia than most Australians did, had met some pretty tough cookies along the way and witnessed how hard life in the outback could be. How we infused that into the Shakespeare play is beyond the scope of my recollections, but it must have had some kind of influence. I should add that the Aborigine people we came across had a great sense of humour. For example, I met one of the guys who was comfortable living in the city environment when I went back to Oz a few years later at the World Expo in Brisbane during the bi-centenary celebrations. He was wearing a printed tee shirt which declared: *Australia 1788-1988. Two hundred years of tee shirts.*

AFTER SYDNEY AND MELBOURNE WE HAD A showdown with our sponsors, the Festival of Perth, who were running out of money. It was acrimonious, and it spoiled what had been a good-natured start twelve months before. When the tour ended in Sydney on our second successful visit there in April 1986, we sold a lot of stuff, including personal belongings, at a big yard sale. The Suzuki motorbike that had been my constant companion throughout the tour went to new owners, and I never owned another motorbike after that. I can't tell you why and I'm surprised at myself, looking back, because the Suzuki 185 will always be a big part of my memories of Australia. I suppose it was the whole easy freedom of the thing, jumping on the bike and tearing off to get the shopping or heading to the beach, compared to the hours and hours chained to the truck's driving seat for thousands of miles around this vast continent.

The rest of our stuff went in a container by sea back to Lisbon. When we split up and all went separate and very different ways back to Europe, we weren't sure where the next base was going to be. For the next few weeks anyway it was 'time out'. Marie and I looked at flights across the Pacific and decided to go island-hopping from New Zealand to Fiji, where she had some friends we could stay with, and then to Taveuni where the date line goes through the island and you can straddle it and have one foot in Sunday and the other in Monday.

From Fiji we took the weekly flight to Rarotonga in the Cook Islands and the tiny atoll called Aitutaki. On to the exquisitely beautiful and very expensive French Society Islands, Tahiti and Moorea. Then across the vast Pacific, north to Hawaii and Maui and finally, after weeks of serendipitous wandering, on to Los Angeles where it was hard to readjust to anything resembling normal life as we had known it before setting off from Sydney, another world away. It turned out to be a journey of a lifetime, full of wondrous sights and welcoming people

Joe and Gio
(photo: Marie Allen)

and it was a real eye-opener to see these lovely South Sea Isles at a critical time, when global changes in trade and climate were imminent. But that's another story.

Back in Europe, 1986

A base in the south of France again sounded promising but the location, north of Montpellier at a small town called Lodève, wasn't popular with the group. I never liked it, and it still gives me the creeps when I think about it. The house and grounds were pleasant enough, but maybe the story I'm going to tell has a lot to do with the feelings I associate with the place.

Initially, from June onwards, when we restarted touring festivals in Europe again, the company had been doing well with the new show, *Macbeth*. Arriving at the site for our gig at the Hamburg Festival in July, expecting to crack on with the set-up for the tent and all our domestic paraphernalia, I found Joe in a state fit to strangle somebody because the festival had not provided running water or electricity. I could tell from experience that whoever turned up representing the festival production team was going to get an awful lot of grief from Joe in one of his tempers.

However, things changed dramatically when Imke appeared. Looking like a stand-in for the Virgin Mary on her day off, Imke was a vision of innocence, charm and sweetness of nature, totally without guile and wrapped in a package of sheer beauty, with long straight hair halfway down her back, radiant eyes and a smile that would melt an iceberg. This was the festival representative assigned to us. Joe's rage magically disappeared and was replaced by a strange little dance, as he hopped from one foot to the other, gently uttering, 'Ah, erm, yes, well, Imke, did you say? Nice to meet you, Imke.' All was resolved within a couple of hours with the usual German efficiency, and Joe returned to being the jovial character we knew and loved.

Footies didn't generally like doing German gigs too much, preferring the temperament of southern Europe. It wasn't uncommon in Italy, on occasions when we arrived on mass for lunch at a restaurant, that our younger children and babies would be whisked away behind the scenes with great shows of affection which were then amplified from somewhere deep in the kitchens with another round of Italian 'aahs' of delight. When they emerged again in the arms of their gleeful captors, the bambini were invariably clutching something tasty in a sticky mitt and sporting ruddy cheeks that had been lovingly pinched and stroked. Sometimes they would even get fed 'off stage' so to speak. (Could that happen these days with any feeling of safety?)

The German thing was also due to a bad experience in Bochum some years previously. A fire had ignited in a car with several actors travelling in it, caused by fumes from contact adhesive on one of the giant puppets. It nearly caused devastating injuries and certainly left scars in the mind. But here in Hamburg, this festival was one of the best, in my view. It had a bewildering amount of things donated

*Bruno watching Gunga play the tin whistle with his nose
while Imke is also suitably impressed*

by companies from the city and even farmers from out of town, so that children and adults could build their own mini-city using metal, wood, hay bales, tyres, you name it. The disused former industrial buildings on site were put to all kinds of use as theatre and workshop spaces. I was really impressed.

A few of us went to see Margaret's aunt and uncle who were living in Hamburg. We were sitting in their apartment chatting away when, for some reason that I can't explain, during a lull in the conversation, I blurted out, 'What was it like after the war?' Margaret had a look of shock on her face as she slowly turned and glared at me. There was an awkward silence as Margaret's aunt and uncle looked at each other. Then, as calmly and as softly as you please, she said, 'We have never talked about it.' And then all these stories started tumbling out from their memories, almost as if they were delighted to be able to tell someone just how bad it had been, picking up shoes from dead people lying by the roadside as they dragged themselves across the country, scavenging for food and eventually setting up a place to live amongst the rubble of a flattened Hamburg. Phew!

Margaret thanked me afterwards. Well, it was fascinating! Margaret's grandfather was actually from near Glindow in what became East Germany. She and Dave J left Footsbarn after the Berlin Wall came down, and together they set up the theatre company Ton und Kirschen, based in a beautiful sylvan setting next to a lake in Glindow. Daisy joined them to become a theatre technician.

By August we were back in Ireland promoting the show at the Galway Races before the Arts Festival started. (The festival moved to its annual July slot a couple of years later.) The shows enjoyed a sell-out run indoors in Leisureland, across from the Prom in Salthill. The good people of Galway had bought a record number of posters, tee shirts and programmes that year, which meant carrying a lot of cash around in addition to the takings from the gigs in Salzburg and Hamburg.

John and I were relieved to get our respective bundles of cash from company fees and front-of-house sales changed into francs when we got to France.

Ollie Jennings and Padraig Breathnach with
Maggie, Paddy and John in Dublin

The Base Camp at Creepy Belbezet

Back at Belbezet, the house in Lodève where the trucks, buses and caravans nestled on various levels on the steeply sloping site, we could relax again. That was until the entire stash from the poster sales was taken from my caravan. It was about a thousand pounds in French francs. I was so mad, especially because given the nature of the set-up here in the countryside, well away from town, it had to be someone we knew. When the base was established a few weeks beforehand, only a few local people were in constant contact with us. There were a couple of guys who found the house for us, who seemed decent enough: a guy called Irish Brian, who showed the initial set-up team around because he lived in the area; a French woman who taught delinquents and young offenders privately at her place at the back of the house; and Joop, a young Dutch guy who kept a horse behind the house.

One of the young offenders was staying with the French woman at the time. Daniel, Julie's father, whose first language was French, had been asking around in the hope of sniffing out any suspects. He concluded that this teenager must have absconded with the loot. Daniel grilled this kid for days, and while he might have been a likely looking suspect, he protested his innocence and stuck to his story. The French woman herself wasn't up to snuff, in my opinion. When her pesky dog bit me on the leg and ripped my best trousers, she just shrugged. In fact, she didn't give a shit about anything to do with us. But I didn't suspect her directly. Joop was a hanger-on who enjoyed our company. He was nice enough, so my own suspicions focused on Irish Brian. Having spent nine happy years living in Ireland on both east and west coasts, I knew Irish people pretty well. This guy bothered me as soon as we met, especially as his attitude changed slightly when I told him I'd lived in Ireland. It was like he suddenly became

The base camp at creepy Belbezet

wary of me. Anyway, Angela and Muñeca liked him and said he had been helpful and cheery, so I didn't push anything.

By the time we were heading off to Stuttgart in the freezing first week of the new year, the mystery still hadn't been solved. I was in the new Dutch left-hand-drive truck, which was a dream to drive, with Bruno for company, while the actors went in the coach. Henry, teaching the children at our school, held the fort back at Belbezet along with Angela and Muñeca. I checked in with them sometimes by phone whenever I could find one. As we approached Strasbourg, where we would stop overnight, the temperature outside dropped to minus fifteen degrees Celsius. The diesel froze, and the truck wouldn't start the following morning. I hadn't experienced this before, so I was lucky to find another trucker, who told me to take the fuel filter out altogether. Sure enough, the filter was clogged with a thick sludge of solidified diesel. So the truck started and off we went across the German border. After a long passage of silence, because I was still ruminating over the theft, I made Bruno jump when I suddenly banged the steering wheel with my fist and shouted, 'Well damn them to hell, whoever it was!' I kind of surprised myself, as it was out of character for me to say such a thing. Anyway, I explained myself to Bruno and apologised for startling him. And then I just let the whole thing go.

After a few grey days in snowy Stuttgart, I phoned back to base to see how they were doing, because a dose of bad flu was going around. Angela answered and said they were all fine but that a terrible thing had happened. Irish Brian had burned to death in his caravan! It was awful. The French police said that the caravan was so badly destroyed in the fire, they hadn't realised there was a body in it for several hours. Ridiculous as it was to suspect I'd had any dark influence on this horrible event, it shocked me enough to make a vow that I would never damn anyone to hell ever again. As for Irish Brian, he was never accused or proved guilty of the robbery, and remains innocent for life everlasting, and rightly so. I wish him God's own rest. But the robbery remains a mystery to this day.

Stuttgart gave me the opportunity to find a replacement engine for my failing Mercedes diesel car. It was a bit of a dog when I bought it, and the compression was so bad it wouldn't start in cold weather. The engine I bought in Stuttgart and took back to Belbezet in the back of the truck was fitted by Henry, working heroically every evening with my help in a shed behind the house.

Sadly, the new engine was worse than the one we took out, and when steam came out of the exhaust, I knew I'd have to get the thing rebuilt. I felt so sorry for Henry, but we learned a lot about the Mercedes, which was good because he had a similar model himself. That set me off on another quest with the help of an English friend, Tim, who lived locally. Together we went to various scrapyards in search of a Mercedes-type 615 engine cylinder head. We found one with grass growing through the hood in Montpellier. In the end, I learned my lessons with that car, and thankfully all ten second-hand Mercedes cars that I've owned since that one have been gems.

WITHIN A COUPLE OF MONTHS, I HAD LEFT FOOTSBARN for good. It had been exactly six years. I felt I owed Marie a decision one way or the other. She contemplated living in Australia again but decided against it and returned to her home town in Cheltenham after the epic adventure across the Pacific Islands together. She came out to visit me a couple of times in France and Italy, wondering what my plans were. She got on well with Footies and liked the whole thing, but she wasn't going to join Footsbarn whether they wanted her or not.

I realised it was serious after she came to France to see me. She joined me in the truck in another epic journey across Spain and Portugal when the container ship arrived at Lisbon docks from Australia with all our stuff. Fortunately, we had help transferring the contents of the container to the truck at the dockside. After another lightning visit to my old friend Carmo in Lisbon, a house where I knew with enormous gratitude that I always had a bed on which to lay my head, we were off again heading for France with a truck full of goodness knows what, but all of it useful enough to warrant saving after sixteen months of collecting stuff by the whole group going round Australia.

One night on the way back across Spain, Marie was in a foul mood because she was tired of not being able to find good vegetarian meals. The raucous noise from the bar directly below our room in the taverna was coming from the local guys playing dominoes and cards, and it was all getting to be too much. She was just about to crank up the hissy fit to another level when the bed we were sitting on collapsed with an almighty crash. All went deadly quiet down below, and I burst out laughing. After throwing her hands in the air, she finally saw the funny side of it. As we tried to put the bed back together as best we could, the guys down below were scraping chairs across the tiles and then they shuffled off home.

Italy in the Fall and France through the Winter

Months went by, and then Marie came to see me again in Italy when we took *Macbeth* to Florence, Naples and Palermo. Palermo was crazy with the sound of police cars racing up and down the streets, their sirens blazing. We were told to wear our cameras with the strap over our heads to avoid having them snatched by guys on scooters near the market, where I was taking photographs of a beautiful olive stall. The theatre we performed in was magnificent, like a grand old opera house. After one matinee show, I was nearly knocked over at front of house by a bunch of Sicilian schoolgirls who demanded to know who was playing Banquo. 'Oooo eez brighta blue eyes, eez goooorgeous.' It wasn't the first time. And they weren't wrong about Rod's eyes.

After the week's run came to an end in Palermo and the truck was loaded up, I was told by the theatre manager that I would have to go to a compound across the city to park the truck for the night.

'Why can't we leave it here at the back of the theatre? It's been here all week without any bother,' I said.

'They know it's full now,' he replied, as if I was an idiot. The compound security consisted of four German shepherd dogs on chains, who looked at me and salivated as if I might be the evening meal. The yard was littered with old trucks, and the whole place looked like it might not have changed much since the Second World War. At least the truck was safe.

I enjoyed our stay in Palermo. I didn't try to find Lucia, because obviously I was with Marie, but I was relieved that Lucia's brothers didn't turn up to kill me. The coach went back to Naples on the ferry with everyone except myself and Marie. Strike action at the port prevented the truck from being allowed on the ferry, so I had to

Olive stall in Palermo, Sicily

drive all the way across Sicily, past the smoking Etna volcano, across the Strait of Messina and on to the mainland at the toe of Italy, and then drive the entire length of the country to get to Lyon in France in time for the next gig. All the others travelling in the bus had stopped at Pompeii, devastated by Italy's other famous volcano, Vesuvius. I didn't have time to stop because I was a day behind them, and I was so pissed off. Pompeii is still on my bucket list.

At the end of November in Lyon, all the cafes, bars and restaurants had signs on the doors and windows announcing, '*Il est arrivé!*' They were referring to the annual release of Beaujolais Nouveau wine. I wondered what all the fuss was about. It tasted young alright, but it was thin and weak, like a wine that hadn't been allowed to mature, which is exactly what it was. Why bother, with so many other good wines to be had for half the price?

Lyon proved to be a really good gig, with a sold-out run and an opportunity for a team of French filmmakers to video the *King Lear* show by using two cameras. After the filming had been completed over two nights of performances, I went to Paris to work on the editing because I knew every second of the show. I realised early in the process that, had I not been there in the editing studio, the finished video would have been complete nonsense. It took hours and hours of painstaking attention to the detail in the cutting room, and sorting out which cameras were able to capture the thrust of the narrative, with all the different characters making entrances and exits, some of which had been missed by the camera operators. Though the editing was a marathon effort, I actually enjoyed it, and working closely with the director was fun. I was pleased with the finished video.

When I got back to base, John Kilby flew into a rage when he saw the bill and immediately got on the blower to Paris to renegotiate the deal (which he was very good at), while I prepared to show the video to the actors. They were less than impressed and said that it didn't capture the flow and energy of the play. While I hadn't been responsible for the filming – the guys had only seen the show a couple of times before they shot the performance – I still felt deflated because so little evidence of Footsbarn's shows existed for posterity. It was largely in people's memories.

Along with this experience, the debilitating long drive back to France from Sicily, and the fact that I was with the group less and less as they did shows in theatres around France by bus and train, I slowly realised that the reasons to make a decision to move on were stacking up. I was struggling to raise my level of enthusiasm to work on the new show, which was going to be based on the book *The Master and Margarita* by Mikhail Bulgakov – a story I loved when I'd read it about ten years previously. My initial publicity sketches were promising, but when I left the company, others including Freddy took over and made a lovely job of the new poster designs.

In the spring of 1987, Rod and Charmian were thinking of leaving at the same time that I was. Rod's father had recently passed away, and change was in the air. After the Mercedes had been fixed with a rebuilt engine at a local garage, at great expense, I phoned Marie to say I was leaving Footsbarn and would join her in Cheltenham in June. To do what, I had no idea.

Bibo came with me, as she was leaving too, with plans to go to school in London. She was about fifteen. We stopped at a place I'd heard about called the Postman's Ideal Palace, to see the extraordinary folly he'd built from stones carried home on his bike over a lifetime of delivering letters. After Facteur Cheval's death, this amazing 'palace' in his back garden in the hills near Valence was opened to the public and remains a monument to him and his long-suffering wife. The following day, Bibo and I got the ferry to England and I dropped her off at a station on the outskirts of London, where she could get a train to meet Jay, her father. Half an hour later, I was cruising along the A339 near Basingstoke when the engine blew up. They'd put the wrong gaskets in the engine block.

Welcome to *Life After Footsbarn*.

The Postman's Ideal Palace, near Valence

And Finally, The End Bit

I saw a lot of Footsbarn shows over the years, from *Jason and the Argonauts* in 1980 to *One Flew Over the Cuckoo's Nest* in 2017 and, most recently, *The Crock of Gold* in 2022. Of those that were in the repertoire when I travelled with the group from 1981 to 1987, my favourites were *Arthur*, *Hamlet* and *King Lear*, in that order. Of those I didn't work on, I'd go for *Midsummer Night's Dream* from 1990; although romance wasn't their strongest suit, it was still an exquisite show.

Arthur suited their style down to the ground and was probably just the right thing at the right time. *Hamlet* with Rod as the lead was also a cracking show with great music. It was no wonder that *Hamlet* was the surprise hit show of the 1981 Avignon Festival and the one that critics said, in spite of the meagre tent setting on a dust bowl site, this was where *real theatre* was going on.

I went back to Portugal twenty-five years later, and after much searching for the 1981 base camp, Joe and I found the site at Baranco with the old farm buildings now in ruins. So much had changed. Great swathes of the eucalyptus forest had been felled, so the views across the valleys looked completely different, like seeing someone you had known for ages with a beard and then suddenly trying to recognise them clean shaven. When I walked down the hill to the walled garden where mother pig had given me the runaround, I found everything overgrown and its walls in ruins.

A slight breath of wind stirred the old windmill and set off the familiar creaking, and that sound stirred up a bunch of bittersweet memories. So I stood there with my eyes closed and remembered the sounds of the children laughing and the energetic power of sixty people working away on the hilltop camp. Just then, the same tinkling bells of the goat herd drifted across the valley, and I breathed in the scents of the mimosa and eucalyptus and the Alentejo countryside. In an instant I was transported back to those nights by the fireside with Dave's accordion, Johnny's mandolin and Laura's flute softly playing, and I could remember being so utterly amazed that here in the forest, with no light pollution, the night sky could hold so many visible stars. What a contrast it had been to my previous urban life in northern Europe, with the traffic sizzling in the rain under the orange sodium street lights. I was so thankful that I'd been given the opportunity to work and travel with such extraordinary people, no matter how challenging it had been. I snapped out of it when Joe called my name, and I shouted back to him up the hill, echoing across the valley, 'It was twenty-five years ago, Joe. It's a third of a lifetime!'

I look at the posters I designed for the company, in my archive now, and the collection of hand-printed ones from Portugal in 1982, and it brings back the feelings of excitement and adventure from that time, but also the angst and frustration from the efforts to promote the hastily arranged gigs that had to be announced and advertised, circus-style, as we went from town to town around Portugal, living hand to mouth. We never got to the promised land of Brazil and Rio de Janeiro. Footsbarn went on to greater things after I left, including the Mir Caravan to Russia before the Berlin Wall came down, and later to India and Colombia and elsewhere. On and on it goes. The company has been based in Hérisson in the centre of France since the early 1990s.

We were baby boomers who thought we'd be lost or blown to oblivion by Armageddon before reaching forty, because the threat of nuclear war never seemed that far away during the Cold War in the seventies and eighties. Yet here we are, some of us still breathing. Others that I worked and travelled with as part of the Footsbarn family have passed on, many of them under fifty: Jamie, Joao M, Spencer, Muñeca, Dave H, Mick, Wanda, Melly, Jenny, Laura and, most recently, Julie's father, Daniel Rovai, an irresistible charmer and truly great clown. May you all rest in peace.

Footsbarn kids, Maypole Dance

For many people like me, reaching their seventies, the ability to see life in reverse is a novelty, so you start looking back more than you look forward, revealing those moments or decisions taken on a certain day, seemingly insignificant at the time, that changed or moulded the shape of your life. In a sense, life is always a mystery, and you can never predict what it is that will spur you to take up an adventure or inspire you to make a career change. For that reason, the time-honoured advice to make the most of your life, or not to throw your life away – a command often accompanied by a wagging finger to many a young person – shouldn't be taken too seriously, in my view. Perhaps a better piece of advice would be a quote from *The Two Gentlemen of Verona*: 'I rather would entreat thy company to see the wonders of the world abroad, than living dully sluggardized at home . . .'

Did I throw my life away when I turned my back on the opportunity to work in New York on animated film? Definitely not. One door closed and another opened. I went in search of a quest: as the knights in Footsbarn's *Arthur* said, 'We're questin'!' as if that was life's *raison d'être*. Do I have any regrets? Sure I do. I'm of the opinion that if you have no regrets, you haven't really lived.

That's not the issue. The issue is being able to forgive yourself. When I recently read the newsletter that I'd written for the Friends of Footsbarn in 1983, there was a glaring failure staring me in the face: I had mentioned the aspiration of having a book about Foots-barn available within a year. It never materialised – at least not on my watch. I was so envious of Els Comediants when their book was published in the mid-1980s. But then, they had a permanent home base in Canet de Mar. We were always moving around, which made projects like that so much more difficult. In a way, this *is* the book I never managed to write, even though it's not a promotional docu-ment for Footsbarn per se.

I ran away with a travelling theatre on a day in May when I was thirty-one, and it *was* a great adventure. It allowed me to experience the wonders of a diverse world from a viewpoint that wasn't just a tourist's. But it also made me appreciate what it was to be European, and that I belonged to a continent and not just any one country. And paradoxically, it made me appreciate what it's like to be a foreigner in an unfamiliar country, struggling with the language and grate-fully accepting the kindness of strangers. To all those people across Europe who helped me do my job with Footsbarn Theatre, I am pro-foundly grateful.

And if I encountered the same kind of people as we were then, whether they were escaping from some horror show in their own country or, like Footsbarn, simply believed they had something extraordinary to offer, would I extend the hand of friendship? Thankfully, I am confident that personally and collectively, here in Galway, my adopted home, we do just that with an open heart and an open mind.

My experiences with Footsbarn gave me the confidence to bring a wealth of ideas and possibilities to the Galway Arts Festival when I became its artistic director in the 1990s. Similarly, I was convinced that the world would be enamoured by Galway whenever *it* came to visit. The relationship has been happily symbiotic. The hero's quest, according to Joseph Campbell, always involves an adventure with many challenges and ends with a return home with a boon of some sort. I trust that if I did return with a bag of boons, it was ultimately all power to the Galway Arts Festival and to Galway city as a mythical place. You never know what will happen when you go questin'.

Home for Christmas by Ted Turton

Principle Members of
Footsbarn Theatre, 1981-1987
(not all at the same time)

Actors: Margaret Biereye / Joe Cunningham / Paddy Hayter /
Dave Johnston / Steve Johnston / Pureza Pinto Leite /
Maggie Watkiss / Rod Goodall

Musicians: Simon Stewart Richardson / Gregg Moore / Paul Nygaard /
Jon Beedell / Dave Rothwell / Randy / Alan 'Gunga' Purves

Technicians: Johnny Arnott / Dave Hayter / Spencer Mead /
Jamie Arnott / Phil Oldaker / Mick Spence / Bruno Hocquard

Administration, Props, Costumes, Masks, Artwork, Photography and Catering:
John Kilby / Charmian Goodall / Fredericka 'Freddy' Lascelles /
Angela Mead / Muñeca Moll / Ted Turton / Alison Arnott /
Laura Ashton / Peter Smith / João Vilanova-Smith / Marta Castro /
Denis Charrett Dykes / Shirley Jones / Karen With /
Caroline Missingham / Eva Jozefiak / Paulo Soromenho / João Medina

School: Wanda Winston / Martin 'Henry' Coulson / Susie Pope /
Jenny Tarran

Children: Josie / Daisy / Julie / Petal / Taro / Bibo / Corinna /
Becky H / Rebecca A / Sarah / Kes / Tiam / Zana / Giovanni /
Amy / Carlie / Nico / Sophie / Alice / Frey / Quillon / Danny /
Melly / Crispin / Rowan

Photo Gallery

Spencer

Dave H

Pureza

Marta

Henry

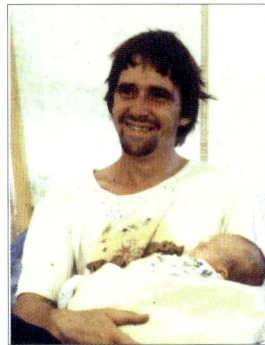
Jamie with Neil

Daniel

Carmo in Siena

Caroline

Marie Allen

*Joe with his
Duncan mask*

Nico

Rebecca A with Daisy

Rowan

Melly

Marta, Suze and Angie

Sophie and Alice making puppets

Kes and Tiam

Josie

Gio

Danny and Sarah with Ted

Alice, Petal and Quillon

Bibo in Portugal

Bibo four years later in Belbezet

Footsbarn Theatre Itinerary, May 1981 – May 1987

May 1981	Ireland Brittany	Galway Arts Festival	With *Hamlet* and *Tall Stories*
June 1981	Netherlands Germany	Amsterdam Freiburg	Met Els Comedians for first time
July 1981	France	Avignon Festival	
August 1981		Aix-en-Provence Foix	At 'Theatre of All Possibilities' House
September 1981	Spain	Barcelona Sitges	Former abattoir site with Cirque Aligre On the beach
October 1981		Xàtiva, Granada Seville and district	
November 1981	Portugal	Odemira Vila Nova de Milfontes Baranco	Base camp in eucalyptus forest *The Devil, the Doctor and the Fool*
April 1982		Lagos, Faro, Serpa, Beja	
May 1982		Évora, Setúbal, Cascais	
June 1982		Lisbon, Vila do Conde	
July 1982	USA	Denver, Colorado Boulder, Colorado Santa Fe, New Mexico	Five weeks in America
August 1982	Portugal	Porto, Vila Nova de Cerveira, Lisbon	
September 1982	Spain	Zaragoza	
October 1982		Valencia, Granada	
November 1982		Jerez de la Frontera	The big break up
December 1982	England, Wales		After new year went to Galway for three months
April 1983	Italy	Turin	New downsized company
May 1983		Volterra	*King Lear* creation
June 1983		Modena, Asti, Santarcangelo	

Footsbarn Theatre Itinerary

July 1983	France	Avignon Sophia Antipolis	
August 1983	Italy	Florence	Festival di Balocchi, Botanical Gardens
October 1983	France	Rome Saint-Stiffret	Parco de Daini, Villa Borghese Base at asparagus farm near Uzès
November 1983		Lyon and 16 French towns	
February 1984		Uzès Saint-Siffret	Carnival *Chinese Puzzle* creation, new tent
April 1984	Italy	Pontedera	Went to Italy to get posters printed
May 1984	France	Aurillac, Marseilles	
June 1984	Italy Netherlands	La Spezia, Modena Amsterdam	
July 1984	Switzerland	Zurich	Lakeside with Els Comediants
August 1984	France Ireland	Lorient Galway Arts Festival	Interceltic Festival Lovely Irish summer
September 1984	Switzerland Italy	Lausanne, Geneva Lake Maggiore	Holiday
October 1984	France	Paris	Indoors at Théâtre de L'Est Parisien
November 1984	Belgium	Tournai, Namur, Brussels	
December 1984	Portugal	Lisbon, Cercal	Holiday
January 1985	England	Devon, London	London Mime Festival
February 1985	Australia	Fremantle	Perth Festival, new tent, new everything
March 1985	West. Australia	Geraldton, Bunbury, Albany, Denmark, Bundaberg, Esperance	
April 1985	South Australia	Goldfields, Nullarbor Plain, Whyalla, Adelaide	Come Out Festival for children
May 1985		Alice Springs	Leader truck problems
June 1985	Northern Territory	Darwin, Bamyili, Barunga, Gunbalanya	Aboriginal villages
July 1985		Bali, Indonesia	Holiday
August 19985	Queensland	Townsville, Rockhampton	
September 1985		Brisbane	Warana Festival
October 1985	South Australia	Adelaide	
Decmeber 1985	Victoria	Melbourne	Christmas in the sun

January 1986	New So. Wales	Sydney Festival	Phillip Park, city centre
February 1986	South Australia	McLaren Vale	*Macbeth* creation
March 1986		Adelaide Festival	
April 1986	New So. Wales	Sydney again	Great yard sale; shipped rest to Lisbon
May 1986		South Pacific	Island-hopping with Marie: Hawaii, Fiji, Cook Islands, Tahiti
July 1986	Austria Germany	Salzburg Hamburg Festival	
August 1986	Ireland	Galway Arts Festival	
September 1986	France	Belbezet, Lodève	
October 1986	Italy	Florence	
November 1986		Naples	
December 1986		Palermo	
January 1987	Germany	Stuttgart	
February 1987	France	Grenoble	
May 1987		Montpelier	Bye-bye, off to get married (for a while)

Picture Gallery

After Ted's adventures with Footsbarn he returned to Galway to pursue his career as an artist and arts administrator. On the following pages are a sample of some of his paintings. For more information, contact Ted by email at info@tedturtonart.com.

A Fine Day in Connemara

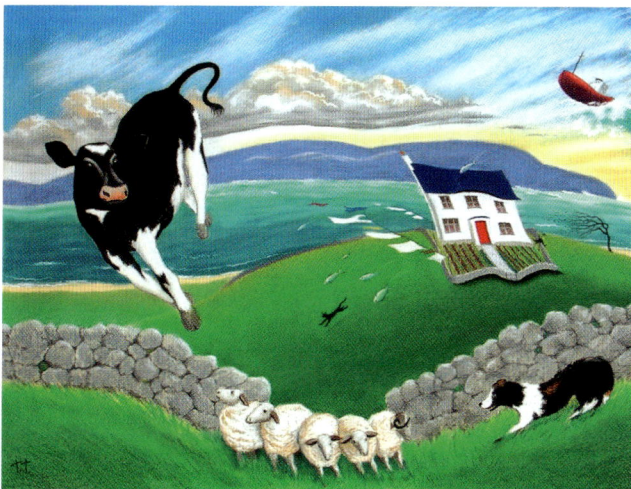

A Windy Day in Connemara

The Fields of Athenry

Cat at the Lake

Noah's Ark passing over Ireland

Nora Dreams of a Galway Wedding (with James Joyce)

Times Past in Kinvara

Ghost Train, Clifden Railway

Roche's Point Light, Cork

Sunrise on Connemara

Home Again in Ireland

Last Night's Dream

The Apparition

The Final Days of Mutton Island Lighthouse

New Year's Day on Galway Bay

Acknowledgements

The first person to champion the idea of putting these stories together in book form was Barbara Dowd Wright, author and mother to my sister-in-law. She has been a constant inspiration and friend and a source of encouragement and belief in me since we first met in New Jersey in 1979.

Lali Morris, my wife of twenty-seven years, whose eye for detail, especially with my paintings, is so sensitised to the detection of 'magic' that she has always been wisely forthcoming, giving me the nod of approval or the nudge to do more, particularly when the magic is not quite there, knowing full well that I am capable of putting it there.

To my brother and sister-in-law, Neil and Wendy, who suffered listening to the first drafts of several stories and enthusiastically drove me on.

To Anne Butler, a long-time Galway friend who, at an early reading at the Clifden Arts Festival, pointed out: 'So many of us wanted to join Footsbarn back in those days; you have an obligation to tell us what it was like, because you were the only one who ran away with them.'

Ollie Jennings, co-founder of the Galway Arts Festival and the one friend that I am most indebted to for an enjoyable professional life spent in Galway, as well as being the recipient of his generous hospitality.

Carlie Buckley, one of the Footsbarn children who set up the first Facebook closed group for Footsbarn members in 2013 which ultimately brought us all together again, and which in turn encouraged me to examine my archive of photographs and delve into a mind full of memories.

The Tyrone Guthrie Centre at Annaghmakerrig, County Monaghan, and all the staff. Much of the text for this book was written there.

Galway City and County Arts Offices.

Carmo Castro (Can I ever thank you enough?).

Carla Pollastrelli and the staff at Fondazione Pontedera Teatro, Italy.

Luisella Casubolo.

Tim Biscombe.

Elsebeth Krogh.

Sergio Vivaldi (died 2021, aged 93) and staff at Bandecchi & Vivaldi, graphic arts printers, Pontedera, Italy.

Henry Boston and staff at the Festival of Perth, Australia.

Stan Carey, copy editor.

My sincere thanks to my publisher, David Givens, for his help in taking this, my first step into the publishing world as a writer.

Finally, all the friends, colleagues and children who were with me in the Footsbarn group at the time who don't get a mention in this book, simply because I couldn't remember a story to tell about you. Thank you all and please don't be too peeved at your absence because you are not forgotten, and perhaps you can foster a sense of relief that you escaped being the butt of my humour.

Credits

All photographs, images and illustrations are by Ted Turton unless stated otherwise.

My thanks to Marie Allen and Peter Smith for permission to use their photographs, and to Footsbarn Theatre for permission to reproduce many images and photographs that I created.

Thanks to the Galway International Arts Festival for permission to reproduce two of my posters.